Praise for *Ed Co*

"Here it is at long last! Ever since Ed Codish first published 'Voyage to Gaza,' almost forty years ago, readers have been anticipating the next poem, the next book. And now this long-awaited collection presents all the poems together — all exploring different Ways, from rivers to mountains. Yet individually and together they form a single and singular voyage to the depths of the possibilities of poetry and its music. This book has been worth the waiting!"

> Karen Alkalay-Gut, professor emerita in the English and American Studies Department, Tel Aviv University, author of many volumes of poetry, founder and chair of the Israel Association of Writers in English, and noted translator of poetry from Yiddish and Hebrew

"Ed Codish's *Selected Poems* shows a life deeply committed to using poetry not to say what he knows, but to ask questions of what he does not know. He uses poetry like the hornworm uses its feelers, to seek out his place in the world. Israeli politics, pigeons, family, marriage, survival: Codish's interesting life in poetry is also a life *of* poetry. His expertise on his life in poetry is a kind of wisdom."

> Sean Singer, poet, author of *Discography* (Yale University Press, 2002), winner of the Yale Series of Younger Poets Prize and the Norma Farber First Book Award from the Poetry Society of America

"The poetry of Ed Codish offers the best, the most engaging effects the art form can possess. His work is inclusive — providing a range of most meaningful themes (first person existential experience, marriage, family life, aging, illness, gardening, philosophical abstraction, mythical analogies, ritual): universal significance embodied in language that ranges from epic rhetoric to the lyrical: his intentions ambitious, archetypal, fulfilled."

> William Minor, author of six volumes of poetry and *The Inherited Heart: An American Memoir*, and noted jazz writer with over 150 articles to his credit

Ed Codish

SELECTED
POEMS

Kasva Press

Make its
bowls,
ladles,
jars and
pitchers
with
which
to offer
libations;
make them
of pure
gold.

וְעָשִׂיתָ
קְעָרֹתָיו
וְכַפֹּתָיו
וּקְשׂוֹתָיו
וּמְנַקִּיֹּתָיו
אֲשֶׁר יֻסַּךְ
בָּהֵן זָהָב
טָהוֹר תַּעֲשֶׂה
אֹתָם

St. Paul / Alfei Menashe

Kasva Press LLC
Alfei Menashe, Israel
St. Paul, Minnesota

www.kasvapress.com
info@kasvapress.com

Ed Codish: Selected Poems

ISBNs:
Hardcover: 978-1-948403-28-3
Trade Paperback: 978-1-948403-29-0
Ebook: 978-1-948403-30-6

10 9 8 7 6 5 4 3 2 1

This book of poems is dedicated to the
two people who most inhabit it.

To Susann Codish, my wife, who confirmed
for me that love is possible

and

to Stephen Horenstein who showed
me that friendship equals art.

Please flourish.

Contents

Voyage to Gaza

All I Could See

After the Tang Dynasty

Homeland, Soulland

Love Poems

Intensities

Humoresque

Ars Poetica

The Wedding Poem

Sailing Past Gaza

SELECTED
POEMS

Introduction

BOOK I OF Voyage to Gaza introduces a mythology that I will use sporadically throughout this collection. It is a quasi-autobiography set in a mythical, symbolic seasonal riverbed, a *wadi* in Arabic. I have not written Book II and prefer to reserve Books III, IV, V and VI for a future edition, one that must contain Book II, whenever that gets written.

The Pigeon Poems, most of which appear here, were written in 2013-2014. I was suffering from crippling back pain and was incapable of descending the stairs from my bedroom to the rest of our house. We have an en suite bathroom to which I staggered. I spent almost all of every day on my back. My only contact with the natural world was what I could see out the window. On the windowsill lived a small family, as I fantasized, of pigeons. They looked in at me and I looked out at them. Almost every day, I wrote a short poem about these pigeons. I came to love and admire them, share in their pleasures as they hatched eggs, nurtured their chicks, taught them to fly. I am far more mobile now, but still enjoy watching these birds and wishing them well.

I came late to a knowledge of the great Chinese poets of the Tang and Song dynasties. Under the influence of Du Fu and his contemporaries or near contemporaries, I studied Chinese poetry and the myths and symbols it contained. I think most of the poems I wrote in response are self-explanatory. I add here only a note about dragons. These beasts are not the dragons of the West, of Saint George or guardians of fair maidens. They come in four species, marked by the color of their scales and their temperaments. In brief, green dragons are friendly but elusive, yellow dragons are indifferent but should not be teased, black dragons are associated with storms and the power of nature, white dragons represent death and must be avoided. The colors also represent the seasons and much more in a yin and yang universe, but I, a Jewish westerner, use them simply.

Many of the "Chinese" poems are exercises in Chan (in Japanese, Zen) Buddhism. They depend on the Chan belief that enlightenment occurs suddenly rather than after decades of concentration. The Haiku, a Japanese verse form, may be the purest form in poetry of this belief, but I prefer the Chinese forms, just because. I have written many haiku but would preserve only one.

> One ash escapes my rake
> and the fire of spring leaf burning.
> First butterfly!

Ed Codish

A note from the Editor

POETICS, SOUNDS, A man's life, wisdom, dreams, sorrows - all
are revealed in this volume of masterful poetry, defying category yet
displaying a rigorous and deep knowledge of what poetry is about.
As the opening Lichtmensch demonstrates, the author sleeps and
"eats" poetry while engaged in the arduous task of honing down
words to essences, leaving a pure matrix of sounds cascading one
after another, infusing new meaning into every phrase. Throughout
this volume, the poetry sings and dances. Between the lines, pregnant
silences awaken us.

Ed Codish is a realist and a symbolist, but behind this he shows
us his love for nature, his courage amidst life's tragedies, and ulti-
mately a strong faith also rooted in the humoristic side of the human
dilemma. We laugh, then we cry. We travel in Codish's mythical
boat *Frog*, placed smack dab in the dry desert riverbed, where he
and his crew-mates wait patiently for the rain to fall. Even in this
parody of our contemporary dilemma, Codish teaches us that despite
everything life is worth living.

Codish takes on contemporary Israel and Judaism in a new and
unusual light, often with a scathingly clear lens, though he never
loses sight of life's amusing absurdities. When speaking of love, he
grows serious, professing deep love for those close to him, both living
and deceased, and above all his wife Susann, his sail in the wind.
Throughout it all, Ed Codish is clear-eyed in his criticism of our

leaders, our values, the shallowness of our politics, our inhumanity to each other, and ultimately our callousness.

Codish's verses have a solid ethical backbone emanating from such varied traditions as Chinese to the great thinkers of medieval and contemporary Jewish thought. He also engages in reflection about his craft and its purpose in contemporary life, while ultimately answering the skeptic's question ("Who needs poetry?") with a blazing answer.

Some poets feel to the bone as if sandpaper were constantly rubbing their skin. Ed Codish is one of them. His skin bleeds.

So how do we receive a man's life work in one gulp? How can we possibly digest it, chapter by chapter? I urge the reader to open to any page and let the journey continue as it may. This is poetry to savor, while one partakes of its timelessness, brilliance and music. In the layout, each poem has its own space and time, while contributing to the unified journey, the Dao, in a particular way. This is Ed Codish's life voyage, filled with unexpected twists and turns, expressed through phrases that haunt and linger. The journey, constantly refreshed and deepened, leaves us exhausted but glowing like the light bulbs he eats.

The choice and order of this volume's sections have been designed to maximize the broad scope of the journey and ultimately the awesome tapestry of Ed Codish's world.

Dr. Stephen Horenstein
Editor

LICHTMENSCH

I eat light bulbs for a living, so
my cheeks gleam pink, grow rose —
incandescent, neon, mercury vapor,
whichever is in season —
the money isn't good; the spirit show's
the main thing, the power bright, the kids
wowed, when daddy pops the bare
hundred watter in his mouth, chomps,
spits out the metal on the floor,
follows the glass with wine, a frothy red,
the juice trickling down my chin,
flecked in my beard, spluttering my nose —
cutting the pour of blood from lips and tongue
so no one knows how daddy laughs and glows.

VOYAGE TO GAZA

Voyage to Gaza

OR

Sailing Down the Wadi

An Introduction

Sandstorms all summer, and in winter too
sandstorms, or wasted rains that washed
the mud inside, and a marriage doomed
fifteen years before I'd sung and stopped
singing. My dog had died, my children
were deep in death already, their outlines vague
and soon to disappear. My hands were dim
at arms' end and my feet, saving my shoes,
gone. Only mind worked: to treat that pain
and be fit partner for my world I drank,
read poems, raged, labored to make the rank
desert I despised mine while I awaited
a hoped for early end. These books relate
a change of mind and wind, a voyaging
out of Beer Sheva's and grim wife's embraces,
clammy but sapless as a temple whore's
assurances that what gods have jury-rigged
man has to sail. My hands are mine again
and my aging feet shamble towards love.
Reader, if any be, this manual
($28.50 in the mail, $19.00

bought in a store)* and fifteen years of grief
and a bottle shared with ever-thirsty death
and above all, an eye for the final chance
to take yourself away, cost what it will,
is recipe against the errors of hate,
a simple for sophisticates, a draught
I'll join you in — come, let's swig it straight.

1

I hauled the boat I'd built across the sand,
many a summer's work in wood and steel —
the only craft around, and sat me down
by the empty river's shore to caulk seams,
and raise a metal mast. I dug a launch ramp
through the eight-foot sheer embankment top
to the dry river bed, and drove to town
and bought biscuits, dried meat, booze,
a sailing manual, and a road map
(that's all there was) of the Negev Desert
from Beer Sheva to Gaza. And I waited,
by my white wood boat in the sere grass
barely browner that the packed brown sand,
picking gray thorns off a bush, to pass the time.

2

Children, even my own, told Noah jokes
(may bears eat them, and their mothers).
My wife, before she left, taking the house,
the car, the bank account, all but one
of the kids (I made her first mate) screamed

---

* Prices subject to change without notice.

sort of a lot, said I should go to hell
instead of Gaza. I said, Gaza first
and after maybe Crete, or Cyprus.
That was the least she said. I miss her, but
the boat is beautiful, sloop rigged,
provisioned better than the house was ever —
darling, a man has got to do his dreams
I remember laughing, hammering away,
covered with sweat and thinking seaspray.

3

The voyage would, I'd calculated, take
three years. The straight road runs for thirty-
seven miles, but the *wadi* bends
south, west, north, west, back and forth and fills
five or six times a year, then only for a day
or a day and a half. The hours of flood
when water rages white and breaks the rocks
next season's rain will hone are better spent
lying close to shore. The arithmetic
came out three years, thirty miles a year
inclusive of allowance for repairs,
restocking up, lotus eating, Sirens,
Cyclopes, my family, psychoanalysts,
my daughter's wedding, and maybe Circe.

4

Most calmly I was, much of the time, drunk.
Mornings I'd straighten last night's crooked nails
and stare at blurry blueprints, shake my head,
pay off what part I could of bills that had
come in for lumber, sailcloth, the divorce, then

get to work. Fifteen years I built,
it kept me strong, and plane and level accurate;
aware this place, unmoving, wasn't my place
for too long: so I was not unhappy
(blear eyed, striving) in my discontent,
laughed often, really, sometime to the point
of neighbors' stories, sometime at my own
if told or not. Woozily I invoked
the raisin goddesses of dried up streams.

5

Clouds gathered, and they blew away. I drank
two cases of champagne (I had no ice
but wanted to be ready) then the rain,
the first one of that sixteenth winter was
a muddy trickle. My daughter and one friend
(a lovely girl — strong arms, good mind, but strange)
stuck by me. October and November were
wet rock and gooey sand, the thorn-bush bloomed
blue-white, frogs croaked, the women answered mail
from National Geographic which contributed
color film, but wouldn't send me cash.
Evenings we went to movies, we slept aboard,
listened to weather forecasts, watched the sky.
December tenth the heavens split, it poured.

6

As, when Haephestus bangs his forge or wife
so sparks or spasms flare and thunder quakes
and makes our children tense, innocent dears,
but braces those for whom an inland pond
or one six-pack of beer is not enough

to slake a thirst for nature in its rude
sub or superhuman manifestations,
as iron cracks or Aphrodite cries
ear-smashing softness over a wanting world,
so broke the storm. The Arabs from their tents
across the *wadi* ran to their bleating beasts;
in town the Jews slammed windows shut, upstream
Wadi Beer Sheva's tributaries raised
seventeen feet high up, and stomped them down.

7

It was my daughter's watch, she ran loosed-haired
into the deckhouse, an hour before dawn
and shook me and my friend awake and out
to cheer the gale. The stones and planks we'd propped
under the keel were practically afloat,
the rush of rain was lit by jagged flicks
by which we saw white dream stuff foam atop
the oncoming water-wall. We hadn't time to dress:
naked, by lantern light we tightened ropes,
pulled tarpaulins into place, we kissed a lot
excitedly, we roared encouragements
sailor to sailor, louder than the east wind
and, the ship secure, wrapped blankets round soaked selves,
chugged rum and settled down till morning calm.

8

Narrow-prowed and shallow, broader aft,
gracefully she balanced on her rails
waiting her name. In the hazy sun we stood,
thinking. Solid or symbolic, real or legend,
what should we call our ship. My daughter pled

Years and my friend said *Love*, groggy but happy
I suggested *Hope* — we put it off
and swung the bottle (a sweet Israeli red)
against her stern and hugged each other tight,
heard creak and scrape of wood on wood and rock,
saw ease downhill, not far now for the water
had risen high, all my years of work, hear
brief but passionate scream from a slow toad
crushed by our vessel, and we called her *Frog*.

9

We slid down after and we climbed on deck
fast, and set sail to slow our *Frog* against
the current and get the bowsprit straight.
Only my friend had sometimes been before
on a sailing ship and her we made
navigator and helmsman. That first day
was difficult. *Frog* tried to spin around,
turn sideways, which it seemed shouldn't matter
too much, for direction was with the flood,
but it didn't look right, and it made her shake.
(I and my daughter had been to sea
but once, His Hellenic Majesty's Ship
Anna Maria, New York to Haifa with
a rather different crew of Jews and Greeks.)

10

I'd gotten out of shape, during the waiting,
and so by noon each used-up muscle ached;
the women, younger, cut my brandy mug
with coffee and they laughed, working away.
In early afternoon I slumped beneath

the midship awning, happier than I
had ever been, but prodded quickly up
was shown how camels on the *wadi* banks
were getting closer, how the bounding *Frog*
was slowing down, although her sails were changed
to catch, not fight, the wind, and fearful for
alluvial boulders borne down from the hills
behind us, lying to catch the keel,
I ordered *Frog* ashore, in the late tricky light.

11

We had to find a place where rock came out
into the river bed, and ground her there
or stick her in the mud and hope we could
dig and pry her loose before the next flood
wrecked her. We were sort of wrecked ourselves
(those weren't cigarettes the women smoked
and I was lightening the load three ounces
at a time). A Bedouin camp loomed up
in gray-brown felt, tents pitched near a grove
of eucalyptus Zionist pioneers
had planted neither for their comfort nor
for ours; there a road bent towards the steep
but drying stream, a gas station stood
beside it, flocks of sheep, and a grocery store.

12

Against an outcrop, granite, we pulled up
carefully, poles in the ooze to ease the weigh
of *Frog*. I jumped ashore and quick, ran
cable in hand, to wind it round a tree trunk
like a pulley, hailed my friend, my daughter;

we three strained, arms tighter than the rope,
the pain of effort sobering, until
our ship was safe, high above the stone.
Then we rested, tripod, on the sand.
No one had ever visited their tribe
from that direction, but the learned sheikh
determined that desert hospitality
and Arab honor couldn't make exceptions.
We were invited in for bread and tea.

13

It seemed best, despite the precedents
of Abraham and Isaac somewhere near here
but long ago, to say the women were
my wives (they'd buy my sisters and we still
had enough money). My friends, I discovered,
knew Arabic, and the Arabs a little Hebrew,
tourist English and, one old man, spy German.
The guest tent was the finest on the hill
and in exchange of gifts — we slipped the sheikh
two quarts of scotch in bottles labeled
orange juice (they didn't look it, but
nobody asked, just passed them grudgingly) —
received a slaughtered lamb, we cooked some rice,
hired a guard to watch our *Frog* and slept.

14

December eleventh we woke late, the day
was clear. Haze-born, rosy-fingered dawn
was hours gone. The thieving natives clustered
under *Frog* and muttered as they gathered
firewood, but didn't touch her. Both my wives

were veiled in squares of a black shirt I cut
and modestly remained in the stifling tent.
All day I squatted with the tribal elders,
telling of water storms, how desert spirits,
thirsty *jinni* come in from dry wind
had blown us forward, praises be to Allah
and the thousand gods who'd lived here before him!
We all drank orange juice, then what there was,
and my new friends made me a proposition.

15

"A hundred years ago," Sheikh Ahmed said,
"when we, sons of the South, came to this land
where borders were ill-marked and easily crossed
and tariff duties high — a paradise
on earth, such as our prophet dreamt for us,
the sheikh my great-grandfather (may the *houris*
swoon around his couch) built a wooden box —
you see it here, sealed always — told that when
a century should pass, a pilgrim would
come through on a pure white ship of the desert
going towards Gaza (ten decades we
have watched, faithful, for an albino camel)
who'd take his heritage and deliver it
to a man there, for a thousand dollars."

16

The box, a boarded orange crate strapped up,
marked, in fact, Jaffa Oranges: Produce of Israel.
I lifted and I felt that was light. Hashish, I figured;
guns and ammunition would weigh much more,
and blessed his sainted great-grandfather's bones,

mystic traditions, customs' costs and borders,
drug laws, the small but safe dry hold, waiting,
of white-ribbed *Frog*, and told Sheikh Ahmed that we had
probably been born for this, our fates,
the building of the ship, the homes abandoned,
the dangers gone and still to come were all
to take his box. I asked ten thousand dollars.

17

Three days we haggled while the sun stayed bright
above beached *Frog*. Towards the end of the second
week in December, when a darkness spread
east, behind us, we agreed two thousand
in advance, a couple cases laded
from the grocery, three sheep cut up, two
thousand from his cousin on delivery, so
we put his box on board and sat inside
his tent, he with his wives and I with mine
now, drank juice, ate lamb and watched late movies on
one of his sixty-five color TVs.
Persian carpets were spread from flap to flap
eight deep. Sunset of day four he knelt to pray
facing south. I joined him back to back.

18

High water from upstream poured by in the night
although no rain fell on us. The Hebron Hills
must have been a mess. I gave my friend
the money to mail from the grocery store
to the expedition's bank in Tel Aviv
and, easier than the first time for a crowd
of urchins helped us, slipped *Frog* in the full

but not too rapid *wadi.* We made six miles
that day, once we discovered effort was
pointless, that the current did all the work.
At five, when the sun like a dead soldier
collapsed, red, on the last western peak
we, tired of company, found a sand-spit
where we could be alone and talk a week.

19

"We really got away," daughter began,
"there's really nothing here but sand and us
and the junk from the town that's floated down
the *wadi,* the gnats, and sheep and camels
in the distance, and your friend (my pretty friend
was sleeping on the sand on the shady side
of our beached vessel) — it's supposed to be
impossible, especially like this, and
also, everybody says that if you do
it always turns out not to be what you
thought it would be, but so far this is fun
although I didn't like the way those Arabs
looked at me and her and Mom was right
you *are* difficult, but you're a good captain."

20

"Beautiful daughter," I replied, "this trip
(if you had gone to school instead of with us)
you'd know is close as we can come this year
to what great men did, before introspection
taught us that excitement lay in voyages
of ideas — and if you think the *wadi's*
dry and unappealing and full of trash

(no-deposit bottles, two dead dogs, and an empty
case of Coca Cola had been washed up beside us
to lie and fester in the hardening mud)
you've never — heaven save you from it — made
an intellectual search for final things
such as your darling mother seeks while I
more limited in desire head for Gaza.

21

"In cities storms are hated instead of wind,"
pontificated I, remembering,
"and lives instead of ships are lost and souls
broken instead of arms. It just looks cleaner,
sweetheart, and more orderly, for shifts of mind
don't show like shifts of sand — until you're stuck,
mired where yesterday had been clear sailing,
and bends of black opinions don't appear
on cartographic charts. People panic
and throw anchor overboard where deep
water won't hold them still, just slow them up —
a slowness that they call maturity —
weighed down they travel day and night and never
rest, as we are at this pleasant nowhere."

22

Four vultures came, bare headed in respect
to clean the dogs. A pack of jackals snarled
but kept away from the great-taloned birds
(the junk would wait for archeologists).
The cool dry day gleamed on the desert, we
gleamed on each other. It was a forever
afternoon, we three awake and not awake —

just there. We passed the biscuits, lamb and wine
and time. My friend and I excused ourselves
awhile to go and do what creatures
when they are satisfied but hungry, full but still
not totally appeased are wont to do.
Night was the same as light, only darker.
We told each other stories till we slept.

23

"When I lived in New York, a little girl
and not so little, men," my lovely friend
sitting on the deck, her arms outstretched against
Frog's mast, her long legs splayed before her and
her hair ruffling in the night wind, explained,
"would look intensely at my eyes and body
(the attitude was nice, sometimes the man)
and tell me with a voice in which ambition
quavered more than lust or even greed,
how he would make his drugstore into a chain,
or become president of his firm, or how
postdoctoral fellowships from MIT
would make him famous, wealthy and respected —
then dinner, a play, a ride, more talk and bed.

24

"It wasn't bad for a year or two, my fond
parents smiled at them all, they bought me clothes,
make-up, told my cousins of how well their little
daughter did, how when I got married
I'd get to change the draperies the way
they changed their clothes, how everyone was crazy
over me. When I turned twenty my mother

asked me when I'd make my mind up, father
noticed that I sometimes didn't get home
till four AM, at dinner often sat
next to a doctor or a dental
student, though I wasn't ill and all my teeth
felt fine. It was time to leave, so I picked me up
a pilot for El Al, and got to Tel Aviv.

25

"It was the same thing there, I got a flat,
and every greasy slob who'd left Morocco,
Iraq, Canada, California,
was going to be head of a drugstore
chain, president of his firm, or get
postdoctoral fellowships to the Technion
or Weizmann Institute and be famous,
wealthy and respected. Only my folks
were missing and they wrote three times a week.
This way at least the letters don't arrive
and I know where I'm going, down to Gaza,
and after Gaza maybe Crete or Cyprus and
your dad (this to my daughter) seems to have
his fuzzy head on funny, so here I am."

26

"I was a child of three when my then happy
parents brought me to the coast at Haifa
then south to Beer Sheva, put me in
a religious kindergarten, religious schools,
planned to send me to religious college —
it was all normal, just that fifteen years
Daddy toiled away, every vacation

and evenings after work. He was, calmly,
much of the time, drunk, would stand on deck
inviting Mom and us to come on board
but only I did, Mommy went away
and said I should come too. I'm just eighteen
but Daddy's nuts and needs me," daughter said
propped against the side rail, standing up.

27

It wasn't time to tell my story yet.
I felt lotophagous, as I had expected
and wanted to feel. Lying flat on deck
between the women, an air mattress beneath,
blanket above, I watched the stars and chose
for concentration mariner constellations.
Argo, Pisces and amphibious Draco
cruised overhead. Each point of fire was new
that night and was renewed every time I looked.
I didn't care that in Beer Sheva too
the same stars shone, for there we weren't, there
no one had been able to enclose them
into his life, or include his night
in them. That is, for all this, one reason.

28

The early rains had reached an inch or two
into the sand, and grass and early shoots
of desert flowers sprouted up light green
across the Negev. By the *wadi*'s banks
colors were deeper and the grass was high
enough to lie in. Sometimes a trickle flowed
down the intermittent streambed, sometimes the sky

would be less clear. Cold nights we cuddled,
in cool days we dreamed; the cut-up sheep
stayed fresh, we ate a lot of *shishlik*,
for we got hungry often in the bracing
weather of ourselves and the great open
winter of that southern wilderness.
Before we packed, we'd let two floods go by.

29

Late January, and our vessel sped
at flashflood pace, southwest, we saw the first
anemones and ranunculuses, red,
thrust up through desert dandelion which hid
in the spread of yellow petals all the grass
and sand. When storm beat down and wind
threatened to turn us over we could only
fight against the wheel, reef all the sails,
laugh a little nervously and assure
our shipmates that, should *Frog* founder we
most probably would wash ashore alive
and if not, the journey had been good, long
as it lasted. But my daughter cried
and searched the passing coast for where to land.

30

She stood upwind so we could hear her shout
above the howl of air and crash of water
that made earth vanish wholly and with fire
in her voice began to let us know she
was missing something on the voyage we
were not. "Those weeks, that month we spent
resting on the sandbank in no hurry

you two lay in the grass night after night
taking private trips into each other I
could not be invited on. The stories
we told at evening and the golden days
were lovely, but if now we're going to die
it hasn't been enough for me. I want…"
The storm's last blast blew the last words away.

31

Whatever godlets sleep all summer long
under the rocks of the *wadi*, whatever naiads
punished for refusing the advances
of greater deities, or accepting wrong ones
have to lie dry, from April to October
then get drenched in soggy sand and slime
before real winter rains refresh them back
to goddess freedom, must have heard the words
the wind blew by us, and must have understood.
As suddenly as Arabs steal away
after they've put explosives under train tracks
the storm abated. In the brightening sky
neat tents of an Israeli army unit
materialized, and we floated over.

32

Rank upon rank, handsome in the sun
the Jewish soldiers sprawled, covered with mud
almost to their knees. A bearded sergeant
(not as bearded as I, he couldn't have
been more than twenty-one) began to lecture
on the dangers of even the winter sun
that far south, but couldn't keep his men

from helping us land and haul our *Frog*
inside their perimeter and from helping
daughter and friend ashore. They all had been
a month at this encampment doing nothing
but practicing how to load their cannons
take them apart and clean them, guard at night,
play cards and *shesh besh* (*shesh besh* is backgammon).

33

We were all travel weary, filthy and relieved
to have survived that day, especially daughter,
and would have slept soundly on the strand
at least until next noon, but the amazement
of the surrounding warriors wouldn't let them
let us rest until we'd told them how
we and our already not so white ship
had come like a wounded whale, hopelessly lost,
to their wretched outpost in the desert.
They brought us sweetened tea and army chicken
and I told them where to look (I couldn't move
from tiredness) on board for some good rum
to make the tea more potable and insisted
showers first, clean clothes, and then we'd talk.

34

In all but gambling, sex and marijuana
Israeli soldiers led, I knew, dull lives,
except when once a decade they would shift
the Arabs about a bit and then put them back
more or less where they'd lived before, and stage
gameless funerals for their slain fellows who
deserved more epic and heroic ends. (I've served

myself, it gives one time to think, if thinking's
what one wants to do.) I felt I owed them
some entertainment for what they had done
and yet would do for us; we needed food
and lumber and some cloth to make repairs
to galebruised *Frog*, and they had those materials.

35

After we'd eaten, washed and female soldiers
(bridling a bit when they saw friend and daughter
cleaned and combed, lean and rather beautiful)
had taken the women off to dress in khaki
for all our clothes were soaked, the storm had swept
tarpaulins aside and blown the battered
hatch cover off and thrown it far away.
I sat inside the open dining tent
with the unit's officers and noncoms
and over the chocolate milk and thick black coffee
and my own tea and rum, I started to
revive and think what tale these brave commanders
would most enjoy. Their sheltered lives and youth
made me consider truth; they'd find it strange.

36

"Fifteen, now almost sixteen years ago,
when I was your age or a few years older,
I was a philosopher, a deep and constant seeker
after what would make of our brief sojourn
in this heaven-promised land we'd wandered
millennia to find, something somehow different
from what I'd left behind me in New York,"
(I didn't tell them of New York, I might

as well have talked of Mars or said I'd come
like Jonah to warn them to repent their sins)
"and much I read and acted too, became
a leader of our community, worked and prayed,
raised up a family, built myself a home
and taught young men and women to do the same.

37

"We almost starved. On Sabbath we ate meat
in tiny portions, but blessed what we had
been granted. All my appetites I trained and tamed
for higher purposes. I was not as you see me
here before you; I was worse. I wasn't
going anywhere, I'd arrived at what
the books I read said I should arrive at
and I sat — hunched over, flabby, happy
with my lot until I noticed that I hadn't
anything left to pray for and that my praise
of my condition was becoming boring
to family, neighbors, friends, who all were making
money, each other's wives, and growing old.

38

"They were not happier than I, not even less
bored with their brief sojourn in the heaven-
promised land. Too much was given me,
the visions of our prophets and the rewards
offered for observance of our Law, came true.
I envied even Job the wildness of
the voice in the whirlwind, and would pay the price.
All my prayers became pleas for anything
to change the even even even temper

of my time. I began to stop on my way home
from synagogue or school to down a few
brandies or beers, on my knees implore
something to happen, and finally I heard
one evening in the garden, some instructions.

39

"I wasn't really on my knees, I was more flat
out on my back, my eyes were closed, my wife
was screeching that the baby needed washing,
that I was a disgrace, and that if I didn't
get up and go to bed she'd throw a rock at me,
and when I didn't answer — I was hearing
answers to my heaven bending prayers —
actually took a piece of wood that stood there at
the entrance to our yard and with a strength
I'd not expected in her picked it high
over her curly head and with an exclamation
I'd also not expected in her hurled
the board at me. It grazed my side. I bled
somewhat, and startled, stared at where it fell.

40

"Sounds from the sky stopped, I'd learned enough
in the flash of insight that the world compounded
with heaven's help for me. In the formless void
that was my brain then, only that board
slightly blood-stained, crooked, lying on the grass
blades of early summer, a rough white pine
plank I had planned to plane into a bookshelf
was all creation. Gladly I got up
and went to sleep, and in the morning rose

much earlier than usual, and I ran outside
to see that it was actually there.
The plank that she bounded off me was the first
piece of my *Frog*. At first my family thought
working in wood would be relaxing for me."

41

I was, I guess, beginning to embellish
a bit, the board had missed me by a foot
but blood belonged somewhere in my story, so I put
it there. Also it wasn't quite next morning
early that I started to build *Frog*. Weeks
lay that plank untouched where it had fallen
while I, at my wife's insistence and my friends'
urgent advice, sought psychiatric help;
I went to doctors, rabbis, and I read
Freud, Adler, May, Maimonides and other
famous, wise, respected problem-solvers
and also Homer, Virgil and Catullus —
famous, wise, respected trouble-makers
those soldiers hadn't heard of. I left that out.

42

Frog and the women much more that my story
held the young men's attention which was just
as well, for rum and the exhaustion of the day's
muscle and mind-wrenching great exertions
had thickened my tongue. Consecutivity
of narrative became for me almost as hard
as the splintery bench on which I half sat
and half reclined, but more and more reclined.
The Negev sun in splendid rose-pink depth

among the remnants of the storm-clouds played
rainbow games, entered my squinty eyes
and lit up there in glorious incoherence
so that I was possessed the while I lost
all self-possession, and set with the sun.

43

Headache probing fingers of desert dawn
and my friend's soft hand on one stiff shoulder
shook me awake. Around us soldiers (I
was still in the dining tent, no one had thought
to move me or been ordered to, this army
is genuinely casual) ate their simple fare
of bread, olives, margarine and eggs, with cups
of over-sweetened tea. I figured there
was water in the *wadi* for half a day's
voyage, slow and relaxing, but when I tried
to rise, my legs didn't work too well. My lovely
friend suggested staying at the base a day
or until the next flood and she helped me limp
to a tent they'd put aside for her and me.

44

Daughter was gone a week — not really gone,
sometimes she came to meals and I would catch
a glimpse of long black hair in a crowd of khaki
and once she stopped by our tent to say hello
and ask me if I wanted anything. My friend
brought me food; I lay down and dried out.
The base's doctor came; he prescribed rest,
preferably in a hospital but I, five days later
was up and about. Lazarus would not be

famous now if anyone had asked him
when he got up how felt his head and stomach
after Jesus woke him. I have seemed that dead
often enough myself but men and gods
get over it and go on and on and on.

45

A week I rested on the army cot
then interested a group of the Israelis
in ship repair. Damage to *Frog* was greater
that I'd feared — her mast was split, her sails torn,
the keel near broken through and only Sheikh
Ahmed's box unsoaked of all our stores. Weeks
would be needed at heroic pace to make
Frog shipshape ere the winter waned and spring
ended sailing season, for even February's
unreliable, March good for a day at most
of ship-bearing flood. Here at this camp our craft
would summer-over, and so perforce would we
to daughter's clear delight and our indifference;
we were *en route*, so what the way be long.

46

Frog, then, could wait. The bearded sergeant wouldn't
hurry us off as long as daughter smiled
contentedly. We had a place to sleep
and eat, and shade, and burly builders. Within
ten days I'd won fifteen thousands shekels
at the local equivalent of poker and
could have picked up more if I'd been able
to think of what to do with it or if
we didn't need good will and services from

my rather simple playmates. At waiting
I had much experience, those fifteen years
had prepared me well for a time of sitting
amusing the bemused the while I worked
away. Just an armored audience would be new.

47

My lovely friend, alas, was forced to listen
to soldiers who would stare at her and tell
of how, when military service was done, they would
become managers of drug store chains
or presidents of firms, or go to school and get
postdoctoral fellowships to someplace
or other and become famous, wealthy and
respected. The two or three who wanted
to become pimps or thieves were just as dull
despite their honest single-minded lust
for money. (I like money myself, running
a ship's not cheap, but better got when needed
than piled up for rainy days. Rainy days, in fact,
were when it had least use, for then we sailed.)

48

On the whole, though, friend was doing well. Tanned,
taut, her head as toned as her skin, she wrote
the official log of *Frog*, she kept our books,
she sat by me or slouched about the camp,
was daughter's confidante and mine. Our crew
held together on land as well as afloat,
which calmed a fear I'd hidden even from
myself. The summer would be long, the army
base uncomfortable — hot, dusty and dull.

I could take it myself, but I decided
to put in air conditioners and to improve
our food and recreation and if also
we could relieve the sameness of the days
our brave defenders led, I'd do that too.

49

Arranging comfortable accommodations
was easy. Boris, the aging cook, had
been in the Red Army as a youth, had fought
from Moscow's suburbs to mid-Germany
and had enjoyed especially the killing
and the looting. Rape was for idiots
who didn't understand that a moment's pleasure
detracted from more permanent advantage.
He'd hoarded diamonds and rare postage stamps
acquired in the ruins of Berlin
for thirty years (there's nothing to buy in Russia).
Now, with a hulking huge Turkish assistant
he drove to nearby villages for drinks and cash.

50

The prices he was getting weren't good.
During the many summers building *Frog*
I'd wandered late at night about Beer Sheva
half or three-quarters drunk and I'd met many
an unofficial wholesaler, businessmen
from Yemen, North America, Argentina,
who'd known the market well and I put Boris
in touch with them, after we'd agreed
soldiers assigned to kitchen duty should
build us a wooden shack, with windows and

Boris would supply cool air and plentiful
excellent food and drink, and this was quickly
accomplished. By March's muddy middle
we'd left the tent and set up hutkeeping.

51

Only the camp was muddy, all around
the Negev bloomed. Wild chrysanthemums, single,
small and yellow, smothered the sand, their roots
held it all together. In the Negev
Kora goes to Hell in May and comes back
in October. Red poppies speckled the carpet,
gave depth of variation to the otherwise
all yellow flowering wilderness; alongside
the *wadi* was the only green where grasses
took the abundant moisture of the hills
and head high lined the watercourse, but the base
where earth was stomped by army boots was bare
so water collected, like the memories
of the lonely, and sank in uselessly.

52

My black-haired daughter, beautiful, so loved
by now the bearded sergeant that I thought
to speak with her, father to daughter, or
perhaps, captain to crewman, to advise
and warn her how her warm affections could
affect our journey; but every day the two
would weave through the tall grasses to the flowers
the very times when I'd decided to talk
paternally. I'd see the bearded sergeant
flex his beautiful-daughter-encircling arm

and they'd be gone. Wistful, I felt, my lovely
friend said to relax. Often she'd lead me out
a different path than they took and we'd crush
rhythmically a swathe in the chrysanthemums.

53

Before the month was over daughter and sergeant
came in one evening with the base's Rabbi
to our wood hut, whose air-conditioner hummed
over our sizzling steak. I poured three more glasses
of dry red wine into crystal goblets
Boris had obtained for us and threw
three more slabs of prime American beef
onto the white-hot grill. We drank and ate
in silence, strained as the knots that held
the god-eating Fenris wolf about a thousand
miles northwest of here. Beneath his brownbleached beard
the sergeant blushed in bronze, beautiful daughter
peeked at me from eye corners, and I saw
her plate untouched, her pink lips wavering.

54

"Frognauts," the classics student Rabbi said,
"this woman and this soldier would be wed
according to our Law, and indeed I think
they ought to be before the flowery fields
they trample through dry up in the late spring
winds that will burn them brown and crumble them
to ash a later wind will blow away,
for only thus will they in a single season
see stage by stage man's life in this heaven-
promised land and see how glory passes

yet leaves seeds that next year will burst up
and spread in splendor. I know you deem this place
a place to pass through, but it shall endure
longer than your trip, longer than Gaza."

55

"Boring Rabbi," I replied, confused, but
sure I didn't care for his cheap symbols,
"next winter we'll be far from here, these tents
will figure in our history but won't be
our home, for home we have none. My daughter
may marry whom she pleases or just have fun
in desert spring's tall grasses and low flowers
which simply mark our time of passing them.
I'll talk to the bearded sergeant, afterwards
to daughter and to you, and if there is
a wedding it shall be an epochal
event, central occasion, men shall tell time
by it, say that something happened twenty years
before that ceremony, or two centuries after."

56

The Rabbi and my daughter went outside.
I turned to bearded sergeant and I stopped,
puzzled, wondering how to start to tell him
yes, you have a father's blessing on a condition
or two. "What are you going to do when you
get out of the army," stammering I started,
"you will be famous, wealthy and respected
I suppose." But the young man wouldn't have
my sarcasm, and pouring himself a goblet
full of red wine and nicely swilling it said,

"*Wadi*-faring father of beautiful daughter,
wily wanderer from shore to shore, who never
will cease from questing while wind blows and rain
falls five or six times a year, ere I decide
on a career, I'll sail with you to Gaza."

57

Happy yet dismayed I heard the sergeant
assure me of my daughter's company two more
years at least and at the same time tell me
that he was coming too. I'd wanted better
for her, not one quite as weird or wise as this.
What young man would waste his years on the *wadi*?
Either he knew already at his age
the follies of fame, wealth and reputation
or was a love-sick idiot who'd give up
his future for a smile. (One should give up
one's future for a smile but only after
tasting both, so one knows smiles are better
whether meant or not.) Probably best for her
would be the master of another sailing ship.

58

But he was her choice. Without replying
I called back to the Rabbi and my daughter,
kissed her paternally, shook her hand as captain,
my friend kissed everybody, even the Rabbi,
and we began to make our preparations
for the wedding. Jeeps were sent out to gather
soldiers from bases everywhere in the northern
Negev, to Beer Sheva with many thousand dollars,
to Sheikh Ahmed and his people who were

asked to bring lots of sheep and hashish and
camels for racing. Men and women gathered
all of a week, my beautiful daughter's mother
drove out one of the days to look around, she
laughed strangely, threw rocks at *Frog*, and left.

59

The sun in one of his last not over-hot
appearances of the season blessed the day
late in March that daughter and bearded sergeant
were wed. Hilarious women soldiers
all day gathered desert flowers, to bedeck
the bridal canopy, they even found
on a slight rise Negev iris, rare and
orchid shaped. Daughter's sisters sent her dresses,
one went with her to a nearby village where
she ritually immersed and filled out forms
while at the army base I and some officers
came to a final agreement on the general
order of festivities for the seven day
banquet which should follow Jewish weddings.

60

Food was no problem, Boris and the Rabbi
handled the catering, slaughtered Ahmed's sheep,
supervised the week-long white hot fires which
roasted them. Large trucks from Beer Sheva brought
countless bottles of booze and one, refrigerated,
a ton or so of beer for getting started
and later tapering off. A soldier scraped
labels from a nice assortment of
whisky, gin, arak, and then he pasted

more suitable labels on those for our Moslem friends.
Tables were spread around the outside of
the racetrack (formerly parade ground) and
were heaped higher than the head-high grass
with all things good to eat and drink, and flowers.

61

As, when a nymph decides that mortal lovers,
for all the extra passion of temporality
which makes them pour all time into the time,
brief, of human loves, are insufficient for
the long matured and practiced bright emotions
of a semi-goddess who learned love from Eros
himself, and arrays her body in Olympian
magnificence and dedicates her glory
to a fellow godling; as a demi-god repents
the time he's wasted on an earthly maiden
whose beauty seeps from her even as he holds
her to his more than heroic frame
and seeks instead a nymph, a cloudy peer,
so appeared beautiful daughter and bearded sergeant.

62

The blessings said, the marriage contract read,
the ceremonial glass of wine sipped and another broken,
man and wife the lovers walked together
to their own air conditioned shack, Boris's gift,
and the festivities started. That first night
we warmed ourselves with wine and with magniloquent
speeches that my lovely friend wrote down in
the *Frog* log. Next morning we began the more
serious business of the celebration.

The seventeen fine racing camels stood
in a line, near a long table by the racetrack's
brown boggy middle, and by the table stood
Sheikh Ahmed and the Rabbi handicapping
camels while, close-watched, officers took bets.

63

The drunken rabble around us, I would guess
five thousand at least, soldiers and civilians,
were not aficionados of camel flesh
but they had money and they put it down —
five hundred thousand dollars we took in
that day the humped beasts galloped from the base
across the flowered desert, up a hill,
turned two miles away from the *wadi* and
galloped back. As when, on the Sabbath eve
there is decreed a respite for the damned
souls in Hell until the Sabbath's over
and all the criminals and other evil
people there cheer their day-a-week pardon,
so roared the wedding guests, each at his camel.

64

There was no house percentage, every cent
bet by our guests was paid back out in cash
yet we, Sheikh Ahmed, Rabbi, Boris and myself,
did well enough because the race was fixed
as was the second day's, which featured horses.
And there were footraces for thousand dollar
prizes, and drinking bouts, and oratorical
competitions too, and cannon shooting
into the Negev hills, and sheep were roasted

by the flock, bottles emptied a truckload at
a time, and even on the seventh day
almost a thousand guests still roamed the camp
wondering what had happened, where they were,
who they were, and not sure it mattered.

65

Contented I, after the bills were
paid and all the damage fully repaired,
the five dead and a hundred seven wounded
wedding guests dispatched to town by army
ambulance, still had made a profit of
forty thousand and six hundred dollars
which sum lovely friend banked. The year had been
a fate-defying and myth-altering
success, I thought, that early April dawn,
waking to go back to sleep again, arms
around my friend. I'd heaps of money that we
hadn't worked for, poets and newsmen were
constant visitors to the hut and *wadi*
shore where we lived then, and where *Frog* was tied.

The voyage of *Frog* continues in later books, to be published in a later
volume.

ALL I COULD SEE

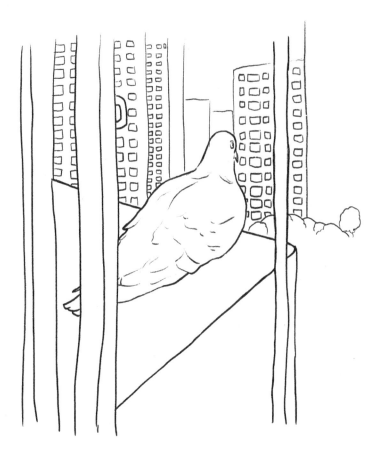

A BLACK PIGEON

It is a pigeon by its shape and bearing
but crow or raven colored. A spy perhaps
but what's to spy on? No crow would perch so close
and ravens are too large for window ledge
and are incurious about inside the room.
How can I write ten syllables and know
the line is done, my students used to ask,
and how do stresses magically align
the way they do in texts? Damned if I know,
I'd reply, and show by writing new lines
on the board, white chalk on green or later
red light pen on white screen. A black pigeon,
unusual, like a trochee in the second
foot, or the fifteenth line in a true sonnet.

A Divine Comedy

And now a dark gray pigeon perches hard,
unmoving on the red tile roof I see,
the angle steep, the pigeon half way up,
a purgatorial bird, unsure how long
the uneven stress will last. It stands and stares
at the mango tree, just now in unripe fruit —
the summer fullness more a- seems than the real
that comes at summer's end. When I looked down
to type he disappeared and now the roof
that stretched from hell to heaven is just red tile
above some sinner's house, and my poor Virgil
to his cooing Dante has had to stop.
Perhaps he rests in mango shade beside
the fruiting date palm, his place perhaps, not mine.

A PAEAN IN PLAGUE TIME

Pigeons on my windowsill are pecking
beak to beak and mounting hard and then
flying, flying, landing with a skid
feathers fluffing under wide spread tails.
The loquat branches bend, heavy with fruit
and the lime tree blossoms. Almonds swell
and scents of Rhaphiolepis dizzy me.
There is the plague. Sometimes I forget.

A Pigeon Poem Without Pigeons

The pigeons have all flown, the window sill's
deserted, the cracked eggs lifeless in their
empty nest. No sentry stands or perches
on the roof. A sparrow image teases, flickers
by and a crow caws in the window's margin,
almost off stage. Swift shadows on the wall
show neighboring nests alive but my flat
landing strip stays cooless. Soon it may rain.
Where do we go when wind and water make
our ledges cold against our claws? Away
like empty memory space, like the empty side
of this bed on this cloudy morning, Susann
awake, phones ringing, someone knocks, morning
is unpoetic, busy, pigeonless.

AIR RAID WARNING

It's only the third this war, in week two,
and no explosion nearer than a thud
behind some trees. No one was hurt, no tree,
even, bereft of leaves. But on my window
sill the parent pigeons lifted silent skywards
and the chicks beneath, their yellow yolk feathers
almost gone, will yawp for food a longer time.
On the red tile roof the lone sentinel
bird has gone, and I return to pigeonless
window frame, but not for long, for already,
food in their beaks, order and world with them,
flapping but silent, knowledgeful, so sure
of what to do. I turn around, I ruffle
old pages, shiver, try to feed myself.

Alone

It is the summer solstice, the longest day
the end of spring, and here, Mediterranean
heat says summer. I'm air conditioned cool,
a brave pigeon struts in the sun.
I know I'm far from home but not how far
because for that I'd have to know
where home is. But like the pigeon,
brown mostly, hopping towards the roof crest,
I'm home, even if a palm
and mango tree and very blue
sky are eternally strange.
My dog jumps on the bed,
does his triple turn, licks me and lies down.
He's home wherever I am.

ANOTHER PIGEON POEM

The pink green pigeon perched on the roof next door
stands sentry on the crest, slow spins around
and never coos. An hour he guards what I don't
know and is relieved. A grayer bird flies
to the lookout post, and pigeon one like a kite
let free first soars then settles on the ledge
of my window.

Another Red Wheelbarrow

A pigeon almost black on a red tile roof
whose eyes are hidden but I name them yellow
in anapestic parallel. Stevens afar
or Williams very close, their images
as much in focus as my actual eyes
except the coo of real, street music just
enough to make me close a book of rhymes
about some worlds invisible from here
without their sounds. A car hums by a plane
if I stretch my ears, and songbirds constant.
White curtains rustle in a whiter breeze,
no twenty snowy mountains, the pigeon flies
away, the red tile roof remains, a thought,
a memory of pigeon coo, a poem.

AVA'S PIGEONS

Flitter through cyberspace onto a ledge
narrower than mine but wide enough
to hold two pigeons, side by side. They stare
through foreign window glass, through camera lens
into a mix of ones and nones and then
by satellite through space to be decoded
and step by step alight, preening, puzzled,
on my computer screen, in this holy land.
They are much whiter than I'm used to,
the purity perhaps of Canadian
winters, of hard sheltering from Manitoban
pigeon chilling winds. It must have been
hard flying. I lie in bed, my hand, real,
extends into a virtual bag of birdseed.

Black Pigeon Reborn

Professor Doctor Rajit after long
and worthy service in two major
universities, master of the seven
sacred tongues, now perches in black plumage,
fat and glad and cooing on a wide
window ledge, reborn this time as pigeon.
His yellow eyes peer outward to a void
between the trees, a palm and an acacia,
and sparrows gather near him not like students
but new disciples, come to learn from him,
the bodhisattva. But universities
like window ledges keep the learned wise
too high, too far above the ground perhaps
for coos to reach and teach us, let us rise.

Blue Sky, Brick Tile Roof, White Stucco Wall, Pigeon

I see all this in a brown aluminum
frame, and nothing else, except gray slats,
straight plastic, in the empty window.
The only motion is a pigeon head
that stops, not even bobbing, and then tilts
in a flat outline away from me, almost
Egyptian bordered, Pharaoh profiled bird
who flies away now, doesn't want to play
this peek-a-coo imagined. I exercise
my legs to left and right, up, down, no stares
outside, my right thigh aches and Susann
pushes hard, the still-life gone, my body
sore and splatted out in bed. I'm out of pills
and pigeons; landscapes don't always work.

Bradley's Pigeon

An artist Facebook friend named Bradley Shaw
has sent me a well-traveled pigeon, tired
as all can see, her head depressed but eyes alert
on a flowering branch in some museum.
Bradley and I have traveled too, I from New York
and he from Florida, I read. I am
in Israel now, he in Montana
and the pigeon a century dead somewhere
in Meiji Japan, or earlier.
Bradley lives in southwestern Montana
and we'd be friends, I think, except for miles.
Freud wrote that distances we conquer
would not exist except for how we beat them
but then I'd not meet Bradley, and I'd want to.

COLOMBIFORM, ANTHROPOS

A pigeon wakes at five this time of year
and is asleep a little after seven.
In midday heat he shelters silently
In the shade of eaves. Or is it me,
following, who wakes and rests and hides?
Pigeons are on my left. Turn to my right
and a night stand with three drawers, the whole
solid cherry wood, and a metal stand
on wheels appears, again three shelves, on top
a basket full of medical supplies
and a folder fat with poems, a shelf below
a urinal and a book of history.
Finally, the day's newspapers, unread.
I'd rather left. Ah! To be a pigeon.

COOED THE PIGEON ...

No nightingale nor skylark, no lurking dark
Poe's raven here, proletarian birds
for whom the poet's me, this rainy May
morning in bed, looking at pictures
Susann sent, an email cross the bed
laptop to laptop. Two pigeons, fat and sleek,
one preens and grooms the other, an orange eye
shines out of feathers, iridescent, bright
as any songster's, and come the revolution
they and their like will rule all window sills
but may allow some sparrows perch room.
I am with them. Up the revolution, down
with pretty poets out of schools; like you
I wave my feather flag, I add a coo.

EAGLES

*My daughter Idit Miriam writes ("ash" is Ashrei, my
grandson and, incidentally, Idit's son):*

*"annnnnnd then yesterdayyyyyyyy when i was really tired
and holding ash on my lap, a PIGEON flew INTO MY
HOUSE and got STUCK, flying back and forth all over
the house, slamming himself into the windows, and i
ran around shrieking the most ridiculous shriek i have
ever made or heard, holding ash who started wailing
because i was screaming, and then i finally shut us up
in the bathroom until adam came home and took him
out (thankfully that was only 3 minutes after i shut us
up in the bathroom). it was wayyyyy more awakening
than coffee, and also some much needed hilarity."*

"Eagles!" we screamed the afternoon two birds,
gray-blue-white pigeons dashed with open wings
and maws, screeching, not coo-cooing but aloud,
eagle-like, into the upstairs bedroom
I sat and played in with my cousin Mike
and toys and games flew faster overturned
while talons slashed and savage beaks sought flesh
or so we thought, our heads so full of stories
everyday reality was impossible
to comprehend. "Eagles" we screamed again
and hurtled down the stairs to parents sitting
puzzled and alarmed until one climbed
bravely up the stairs. My daughter writes that one
is found, after so many miles and years.

Fierce Fowl

They're black of course, and yellow eyed. Sharp darkness
staring down so black descends and sneers at light
and no one dare be literal, call them birds
who are so much more. Look at them back
those beaks mean you and not as friends, will break
and tear in dreams and nightmares. Or are
they guardian dragon feathered beasts
perched hard above, on door or window frame
prepared to fall, swoop like a parent spirit
to bring you back to day? I cannot say,
here in their shadow. I think there are more,
I hear the beat of many wings approaching,
the clacks of claws, the flight of courtyard fowl
and songbirds skittering out of our reach.

Flight School

Both parent pigeons and a favorite aunt
and the two squabs, nervous and close huddled
on the very top of window ledge, hard hopped
to from the nest, touch beaks, spread unused wings
(the chicks) and lean out into air. They see
the swallows, other pigeons, sparrows, all
flapping and soaring, flying roof to roof —
but not yet. Perhaps tomorrow one or both
will drop into that sky, feel lift and rise.
Above three F15s leave jet trail smoke
and flying wing to wing they tear great holes
in the very heaven, turn south to Gaza
to kill whatever stands or walks or crawls
on ground. With puzzled eyes the pigeons see.

For Maya JB Baida

You liked one of my poems then vanished
like a bird glanced flying past a window
and I ran to it, but birds move faster
and in more dimensions than the eyes
grown old. I think you my granddaughter
but how strange to write that. I think you left
a feather. I saw it fall, in the morning
I'll gather it because perhaps some day
you'll want it back. Meanwhile it's safe. It's here.

For My Pigeons (stuck in bed: 5:30 am)

Fat symbols, happy far as I can know
coo-clucking, preening, waiting for my hand
to make them into feathered humanity
before they fly away. I wish some hand
could write me into sign, significant
but puzzling, worth the questions I'd evoke
the way those birds poke questions in my mind.
I lie in bed, my head turned to my left,
and listen to their foreign language,
translating coos to words and words to more
than search for crumbs or sex though crumbs and sex
can fill a world. I think they see me, lying,
staring out. They can't know that they're safe until
I know what pigeons are, what pigeons mean.

Ghost Pigeon

Birds who are not pigeons hop and flutter
across the planter on my window ledge;
an old, old gray white pigeon scolds long coos,
elicits song and silence. The sentry
bird's a crow, my cat's confused. Now evening
chirps and scratchy coos before they settle
and I do not, looking left at nothing.
Poor Susann! She is stuck downstairs at work
while I think bird themes even about the birds
who are not here. And now night settles too
and invisible fowl coo, crow, caw, sing aloud
whether on ledge or deep inside my mind
like all that are missing: words, children, spring,
the work, a feathered head, a sheltering wing.

Gracelessness

Their frequent lack of grace, the bumping wings
to stop a fall, the louder coos of balance
on narrow ledges, even the start of flight,
half clumsy skip before the air and feathers
marry, and lift the bird heavily skywards.
I've come to love these pigeons, slowly they've taught
me they are pigeons, and my tries at more
are either folly fancies or my own
colombomorphic hopes. Birds lack no grace,
and coo's not fall or balance, and the skip
is how a pigeon always starts to fly.
But then the window dims and only nature,
a shadow's shadow, a boredom 'til I sleep
and see my clumsy friends, like me, off balance.

Heat Wave

Perhaps too hot for pigeons on the sun
absorbing stucco or concrete ledges
I can see from here, in bed, all twisted
towards where pigeons perch on cooler days.
It's early afternoon, the breezeless fronds
and mango branches move about as much
as mind would if not lifted and informed
by inside winds, brain tossing motion mixing
the landscape's stillness and its birdless now
with maelstrom thoughts. But a pigeon head just pokes
a purple blotch, shining, and makes a meaning
where otherwise was false, just me imagining
no motion into thought. And now that head
retreats, all thought is gone, and the heat remains.

Hello, Hello: Pigeon Chicks on My Window Sill

Two pigeon chicks like hungers yellow flecked
hatched yesterday because the empty world
needs life and flight and guano, new feathers
flapping, rising, eating, cooing, fucking,
laying eggs and loudly waking us,
not yet but soon. I've come to love them,
my cooing this, poem after poem,
insistent I'm alive, as they are, voiced
if small, no nightingale or swallow
but song and song we screech and warble out.
They are annoying, yes, but not to me
nor I, I think to them, our messy lives
at least are lives, like pallid pink is color,
a cut log dragging on sandy soil a sound.

Hissypus and the Pink-gray Pigeon: A Fable

Fwap fwap of wings against the glass
a deep growl, swipe of paw and click of claw
and quick glare before a brief retreat,
and no engagement, ceasefire but no truce
in a window of no opportunity.
This hate is beautiful, nature arranged
so creatures act their will as harmlessly
as playground children, huffing horrors out
of what they'll do tomorrow. Watching I
now lift a sharpened stick with carbon point
above my paper, or strike keys against
an unresisting board. So now tap tap
of finger tips against fierce mocking words
and the nameless wall that always guards us.

STILL LIFE WITH NASTURTIUMS

I am lying here in my mind and consider
my brain, all those books and movies I've read
or seen, and the random sounds of New York
and Tel Aviv, Wisconsin, not as many
in winter when snow mutes everything
or classroom whispers, and the random non-mind
thoughts that don't connect me and the world.
Brain is what's now, the taking in, the flowers
on Susann's dresser, the color, scent and shape
of each nasturtium, itself and mirrored
into bouquet, red, yellow, orange, almost
white. They cluster in a wine glass. My mind
imagines Susann bent to cut them just
a thought out length. I raise the glass in a toast.

Making Room

Sometimes they squabble. These aren't doves of peace
and the window ledge is narrower than two birds
who aren't making love. The rapid flap
for space enthralls the cat who leaps and claws
the screen, which catches him in flight and breaks
the quarrel and makes two pigeons fly, a pas
de trois, then quiet, the cat away, the birds
back to some other window ledge. I clap
at the performance, at all such, around
me every day, all hours, the curtains
blow back in barely breeze. Ziggy my dog
unstretches at my feet, adds depth of field
and left of this Susann types and sometimes pushes
my arm away for space, and I make room.

A MAROON-BREASTED CROWNED PIGEON

Ava Block-Super a friend I have never
met in the flesh emails me from afar
a pigeon she too's never met I think
in the feather, Ava in Winnipeg
I in my Israeli room the pigeon
spectacular, perched in a jungle somewhere
in New Guinea. But is this a pigeon?
I'm no ornithologist, my pigeons
nest pink, gray and black just outside on a ledge
of my window, uncrested, just like all
of their kin, local and real. So virtual
birds flock near virtual me, sent by a
virtual Ava from a virtual
land. I hear laugh and a coo from outside.

MOT

Are pigeons Jewish? They must be, I think,
so visible and loud, so very common
and to cultured folk, small song birds warbling,
their coos and gurgles crude, their ugly nests
and fetid droppings covering the ground
and hoods and trunks of cars reminders that
they too are birds, that pigeons, puffed and fat
are more like us than comfort might allow.
We build our house with pigeon sills and eaves
and drop crumbs as we eat, pass pigeon food
as if to cousins, dusty, tired from flights
to safety here, flapping and fluttering
brash, uncouth, so loving each with each
we call the white ones doves, we call them peace.

PIGEONS, TOO

Not only pigeons flap around my brain
but I prefer them, dirty, squawks and coos
and mindlessness. No pigeon thinks or worries
if this is all there is, a summer ledge
to perch on, warm and safe and high, an eave
above so hawk can't see and on a wall
unclimbable by cat. I toss them crumbs
to keep them, watch the gray and purple pink
and shining iridescent rainbow plumes
that are not art but nature. Pigeons shit
all over Susann's car, their wings enrage
our Hissypuss the cat who killed one just
two weeks ago for fun, and not for hunger.
I love them, savage, safe, and so not me.

The Pigeon as Lana A.

I know how order is maintained throughout
my towers, how the scurrying streets look down
or across the water. How many days
and darknesses I sleepless perch on stone
peaceful as my white sister but prepared
loudly to coo and swoop, flocked or alone
on what to you appears a scrap, a stray
crumb of old cracker or a rumor wrap
I'll pass encoded later in a drop
white coated dark inside and that may fall
on diplomatic sleeve and start a war.
Except for raptors, pigeons aren't chased
for long. The unsigned contract, ages gone:
I keep the peace for peanuts, and don't tell
any more pigeon poems for a while, unless they force me.

Palm Dove

A pigeon shelters on my window edge —
a palm dove, really, to be accurate,
but in New York it would have been a pigeon,
a deep pink pigeon with a purplish head,
a little unusual, an observant child,
to get attention might, slightly raising
her voice, say, "Look at that pigeon." No one
would respond with more than, "Yeh." There would be snow
rather than this rain, the clouds would move
more slowly in a somewhat lower sky
and the wind's speech, sharp in the leafless trees
would be less guttural, there'd be no scratch
of frond on frond. We would be ten years younger
and our fingertips, touching, a little softer.

PIGEONS

They wake me cooing on the window sill.
I think they wake the rooster down the street
who yawns and then confirms that it is day
loudly and well. And now two eggs speckle
the planter where flowers died. She crouches
careful. Who needs more pigeons? I could reach
out and thumb them to the brick paved lot
below, but I do not, because they are alive
or will be. I vote pro-choice; if she should
ease eggs across the edge I would not blink
or think less of her. But she won't. They never
do, and we'll watch feathers sprout as maws gape
wide, then fluttering, flying, then two pigeons
more, and noise. Maybe next year I'll be smarter.

Please Come Home

What if there are no pigeons when a pigeon
would make a poem? The empty roof eaves,
blank birdclaw empty window ledges
are like white paper, clueless what to say
in words or coos. I take a half a slice
of breakfast toast, the heel end, break it up
to small and smaller bits and sit and chat
with Susann, pet the dog who curls and licks
my feet, unshod, beneath the dining table
and long for pigeons to make me start to sing
in person voice. I ask the woman by me
please to strew the crumbs I've made outside
for pigeon feast, an invitation to
my fellow poets, poems word and coo.

Preface to a Mystery Series

Wings Flap at Dawn, or how about, The Coo
that Caused the Crime, or even The Squeaking
Squab; I'm trying here to find a snappy title
for volume one of what will someday be
the pigeon mystery series, one in which
a wise old bird, too old to fly, who perches
upon a slab, a gray stone firmly placed
under a large glass window, curtainless
with open shutters so the master peers
inside and out, knows fowl and human both
in all inequity, perceives how sparrows
steal and crows deride their betters, people
eat eggs and fight abortion, hypocrites,
eat chickens, ducks, and sometimes each other.

Yeah!

Shelley had skylarks singing while he wrote
a glass in hand, and Yeats a Godly swan
or golden bird, Catullus just a sparrow
but it hopped on girlfriend's breasts until it died
and Poe is famous for one nightly raven,
Keats for a nightingale he never saw
but heard. I — only pigeons, proletarian
fowl who befoul the plazas of the world,
are chased on city streets and have no song
to pleasure human ears. It seems we choose
each other, they and I, not wholly plain
but somewhat fancy plumed, can strut and coo
puff out fat chests and fly, not high and swift
but sure, insistent, here, and unafraid.

Shelter

Doves may be pigeons but their whiteness
like the dare of a white page, just like
the unexplored rebutting and attraction
of the unwritten, the must be written,
around us all gives coo and cause, a sound
and also why to words. The wind of words
blows tempered through the dovecote, sometimes breaks
away from sense, or ruffles feathers, prismed
by the sun. Already, voice and color,
meaning almost assembles, these signs of peace
that join the sheltered birds. The nuanced coo
is nature overflowing into a world
it does explain, but not in any tongue
we can configure except when joined with ours.

Susann's Asleep

March 26, 2014

Perched on the roof next door the pink green pigeon
stands sentry on the crest, slow spins around
and never coos. An hour he guards what I don't
know and is relieved. A grayer bird flies
to the lookout post, and pigeon one like a kite
let free first soars then settles fluttering
on my window ledge. Cat Hissypus aware
of this change of guard seems to approve.
Susann's asleep. I watch her breath inflate
then drop a blanket. I lie still trying
to puff pattern into thought, a pigeon flight,
cat quiver, Susann stir, the sometimes turn
of page I read, the blue sky dimming now
and the quiet, the silence of my mind.

Hunger, Anger

The pigeon chicks are hungry, or better say
are hunger. And the terrorists of Hamas
firing rockets blindly at my pigeon
sill, bechicked and open-mawed, unarmed
civilians, as am I and Susann, are anger
itself. We answer ten for one. If only
they were angry they would stop, the payment
back too much to bear, but there is no food
enough to sate. The chicks may grow full fledged
and fly away, be satisfied with what
they gather, grown, but what will fill the need
of anger except blood? Poor chicks, poor us,
but poorer most the anger filled who die
screaming their need, that terrible hunger.

EVENING

The pigeons all have flown or spread a wing
over their nestled heads. Competing chirps
from swallows, sparrows and some hidden bird
behind a palm tree, and a louder call
from an untended car alarm, white
hooded, wingless, glassy eyed, but owned
like no night bird, no owl waking now
to hoot and hunt, pretend that nature seeps
out of old English books, Shelley perhaps,
an embarrassed skylark wondering if
"wert" is a word. Hissy my cat perks ears
but knows by now he can only hear
that snack fly by. Night and I turn to Susann;
books, the computer streaming television.
The pigeons have all flown, the window sill's
deserted, the cracked eggs lifeless in their
empty nest. No sentry stands or perches
on the roof. A sparrow image teases, flickers
by and a crow caws in the window's margin,
almost off stage. Swift shadows on the wall
show neighboring nests alive but my flat
landing strip stays cooless. Soon it may rain.
Where do we go when wind and water make
our ledges cold against our claws?

THE ROMANIAN NAKED-NECK PIGEON

A Romanian omelet begins,
an Israeli joke starts, with "steal two eggs."
Here is a whole stolen pigeon, Romanian
or not, depending on Transylvanian
winds. He once perched on my window ledge
but stands now on some plastic cylinder
in a tilted monitor. Where he forced head
through window screen white feathers flecked with beige
make downy heaps Israeli birds will gather
to soften nests. In thanks to Steve who guided
this pigeon here, I have already taken
fourteen fine feathers and I hold them here
in comfort, stroking my aching legs, watching
through them the Balkan sun and feel that wind.

TWO PIGEONS

On top of Eitan's window, a thin white
stuccoed ledge below the brown aluminum
eave, cooing, two pigeons love each other.
The place has long been pigeon bare, Eitan
too has moved and the empty room saddens me
without a need. My cat sees pigeon sex
and lays his ears against his head and curls
his tail into pre-leap, but the window
stays him, a win for the erotic over
the hunger of a well-fed cat. Both birds
are pink and gray, a shining purple round
their necks. One is much fatter, wait, a flutter,
and both are gone. So is my son, no pigeon,
but I want full windows, I await returns.

BIKUR CHOLIM (VISITING THE ILL)

After three days of lying pigeonless
in bed this morning early on the ledge
of my window, sit two pigeon friends, one
almost black the other pink-purple gray
and shining, both yellow eyed, they bring
comfort and distraction. Susann gets up,
they startle and depart, their flapping wings
alert a third, above, to fly away.
It is religious law to glad the ill
but who thought pigeons knew this, in their air
and ledge and branch all natural life of nest
and egg and flight and staring in at me,
writing about them, making pigeons a part
of human life, like we all make each other.

AFTER THE TANG DYNASTY

"Do Not Go Out of Your Gate, Sir!"

Li He (790-816 CE)

"Nine headed serpents devouring men's souls,
snow and frost snapping men's bones
snarling dogs, barking
hunt us down,
licking their paws..." and more like this
on the other side of the jade gate of Eden.
Yet here as there birds sing
and roses flower, lavender
scents the spring air, when frost melts,
and the sated serpents feeding on the dead
although they've eaten most of those I loved
have spared me almost eighty years
and in their terror size and thunder growling
point me the Way to unapproachable Eden.

A REAL GREEN DRAGON

NASA just released a picture of mysterious "dragon" aurora
rearing its head in the sky. You can see why our ancient ancestors
believed in mythical monsters and magical beasts.

This dragon is not myth or magic
real as any poet, I see it rear up and hear
through mind to mind a roar
as loud as dream scream, mute
except to the dreamer. Pictures don't lie.
The calla lily in the garden
in front of the unblooming rose bush
cannot exist in memory
but lasts in words. The green dragon
always governs the heaven
that shrinks away in fear.*

Many Chinese dragons are friendly, a few are nasty, and most just don't care
about you. Green ones can go either way: you can make friends with them, but be
careful about poking them. Let sleeping dragons lie.

A POEM IN PLAGUE TIME

It isn't news we're all going to die
like always, surer than the news
the white rose bush will bloom again
or that my back will hurt mornings before
I take my pills. The President of
the United States may say it's fake
news like reports the plague is uncontrolled
or that he is like Canute, the Danish king
ordering the tides to cease their unremitting
assaults on Danish soil. The argument
is over what we'll die of, age or plague
or accident, or by our own devises.
Standing erect I watch the white rose climb
the stony fence. My back anesthetized
I count the twenty buds. That news is real.

A QUIET NOON WITH PAYAM
AND FRAJDA THE CAT

Sitting on the concrete patio under a sun shade
after reading Du Fu I write this poem in English
next to me Payam, after reading who knows what,
inscribes poems in Persian, ghazals he reads us;
ears back, tail straight, teeth forward
cat hunts a bulbul, easily flying away
like the words do as we search for them
the sun high, chirps, the barely heard
sound of rose petals unfurling.

A SONNET FOR YINGLONG, A WINGED EARTH AND WATER DRAGON

Under the earth Yinglong adjusts the drip
of water, fertilized correctly just
to nourish roots. Yinglong has wings to fly
where water gushes from the rocks, but here
tends to our roses, makes the almond bloom
in early spring. Pagans had dragons, spirits,
demi-gods, but I have computerized serpents
slithering and slimy, wet as blood or tears
salty barely on my testing tongue. A thousand years
to grow those yellow wings, ages to form fangs
and cultivating claws, all for the rose's week
the lily's day, the butterfly whose summer life
I watch, while dragon mist is most imagined
the breeze of beating wings cools my red face.

"Long" is the Chinese word for dragon, and "Yinglong" is a rain deity.

An Honorable and Respected Old Age

Rain inundates our garden, washing out
traces of all young dragons
turns Phoenix ashes muddy, mystifies
and mythifies my mind, approaching eighty years
of circling the sun, under heaven. The soil is high
above any flood plain. We are safe.
Honor and respect elude me. One child is worlds away
not just in space, a seed carried
by evil winds to alien beds
of mostly weeds the songs from there
lie by my bed. I do not think I'll read them,
though I taught many how to sing.
My body used to give me pleasure.
My teeth are dental plastic. I cannot walk
as far as I can see. Only narcotic drugs
let me sometimes think
the way I once thought better.
I have dispensed and spent my wealth
such as God granted me. Sometimes
a yellow dragon banks his orange fires
and licks my hand. Women still attend me,
daughter, wife, a friend, granddaughter. My garden fills
with roses, even now in winter.
I don't know when this poem ends
or what I'll say then.

An Immortal Bird at My Window

A brown pigeon stares at a pale gray sky
waiting for winter rain perhaps
on my wide windowsill, watching me read Du Fu
maybe remembering when Du Fu
ages gone once saw him
far away across a bamboo forest.

AUGUST HERPETOLOGY NOTES: THE GARDEN HUMS

A dragonfly hovers over a purple Angelona
three real dragons watch
two under cooling leaves in the hot day
and one all white high in the palm tree
humming with the palm doves.
They are my friends unlike
the great coiled monsters of my dreams
and in my long poem "Voyage," beasts
I've had to slay, reptiles St. George
would flee in horror. Glittering,
beautiful, silent and fireless
the dragonfly swerves to the blue Hibiscus.
Huanglong nods familial, an older brother.

"Huang" is the Chinese word for yellow, so that Huanglong translates as yellow dragon. The yellow dragon is essentially friendly.
No dragon in Chinese tradition has any relationship with the large reptile killed by St. George. Had that Christian gentleman encountered a white dragon, he would have done well to run for his life. One fiery breath would have melted his silly sword.

Dragons

Dragons live in the garden
and in the sky, dragon black now
in early afternoon. Black dragons, winged,
fiery tongues flaring, the deafening roar
when dragon smashes flaming into dragon.
Below, our yellow dragon deep ensconced
in December fallen leaves, drinks giddily the streams
of rain that fill the soil, and grumbling, still asleep,
a green dragon is invisible except the rustle
of covering leaves, scraping,
against her scales, and the white stone fence
hides all sign or symbol of the terror
white dragons are, swirling and jeering
down Paratrooper Road, like tanks, like war.

DRIVING HOME AFTER AN OPERATION ON MY CHEST

Turning at the entrance to our house
swallows swirl as if disturbed
forked tails fly in a gray metal sky
before and after rain in rapid wind
to the fruit heavy branches of the loquat tree
and I limp to the brown wooden door.

ED CODISH READS THE NEWS, JUNE 2019

This Is What's Happening Now

A sunbird landing shakes the pink sage
Susann is planting annuals
honey bees watch and a white butterfly
a Persian friend writes a ghazal
the sunbird sucks the nectar
from one flower, then another, hovering
before she disappears in the blue flowers
of the looming Duranta. I show all this
to my dead Mother, sitting with me,
the scent of red roses barely in the breeze.

For My Sister Sheila, Dead at Twenty-seven

The gardener trims branches from the tall Vitex
and they fall into your shade, a thought of you
on the path we made, heaving heavy stones
quarriers carved just south of Bethlehem
and sold to our stone mason working in a village
of Arab citizens, and sold to us
smooth polished but unwashed of all the souls
that walked here, and perhaps drawn to souls
my sister joins them. I shall know her walking
in my garden, on the invisible Way
behind the tall Duranta, always out of sight.

HAIRCUTS

Clip clip pruning the yellow flowering Senna
all the way to the yellow dragon soul,
the warning snarl of the serpent
awakened now by shears slicing sharply
to the reptile spirit at our transcendent core
hidden under the beauty of this world
and I see my son-in-law preparing
my grandson's first haircut.

Huanglong Hides and Creates This World Now

Huanglong that yellow scholar dragon
inventor of writing, that accursed art
that makes me turn again from field to page
scratches her scaly belly on the rocks
we used to write a path around Nandina
and gardenia flowering Tabernae the beast
just barely seen, a comma perhaps
hidden in the deep wooden shade
as wisdom hides, the difficult art
inscribed on nature, yellow dragon made.

Huanglong Lives Under the Senna

Huanglong, a yellow scholar dragon
coiled scaly side to frond scar
around the tall palm, climbing six feet
up the twenty foot trunk
disguised as a Senna, yellow flowers covering
the reptile's body, writing and writhing
as the gardener's shears
uncover the spirit beast
and a white dragon appears
as the soul of the Nandina.
It is mid-August here.
Dragon's heave their flanks in the heat.
Most are illiterate and oblivious
animals in the heat of summer
growling and hissing with the wind,
ill-meaning fires and thorns
I tell Huanglong.

I AND A DRAGON ENTERTAIN THE DEAD

Sitting half asleep staring at the garden
stoned still from last night's too much
a sunbird flies wing twirling and two butterflies
ignore the Dao I've plotted and seen planted
between the tall Duranta and the Leucophylum
all blue flowers rimmed in white
beyond a new planted shrub across the Way
the usual ghosts stroll and grimace
unhappy dead. A green dragon stretches
yawns, but keeps the dead away.

"I DON'T TAKE RESPONSIBILITY AT ALL."

President of the United States Donald Trump

Zhu Zhanji, the The Xuande Emperor
fifth Emperor of the Ming, in 1430, said
"I am responsible for all under heaven,"
and of his reign was written
it was a golden age, the Chinese nation
lived without wars, the very name Xuande
"Proclamation of virtue."
I am responsible myself
for every evil, for every man and woman
crying unheard when I have ears to hear
and hands and mind. I lack Zhu's dragons
and the thousand horses, and the billions Trump
hordes sneering. He is not himself
responsible for anything. Woe to the nation.

I Stop to Smell My Night Garden

At night when dragons sleep
stormless silence, stars visible
even near cities, in my garden
sweet scents release themselves to waft
enticing me to step into the dark
like Adam offered fruit of a certain tree
that might be out there still, waiting.

I TRY TO THINK BUT MYTH INTRUDES

Even after Enlightenment and science
the knowledge of cause and effect
the Linnaean consequence of genes
connections traceable to Creation
I still know the yellow Senna blossoms
on the great plant tightly coiled
around the base of the fifty-foot-tall palm
are dragon scales, the sleeping beast
protecting genius of the summer garden
puffing heat bubbling fire
peaceful to us. Under the Datura tree
heaps of yellow poison. On the Nandina
red berries can kill birds while the white flowers nourish.
Myths mix with myths and science
I see the yellow dragon stretch
sweet scented scales cover the walk
the Phoenix, returned, stretches ashy wings.

IN ABOUT THE YEAR 759 CE, WANG WEI DISCERNS THE COLORS OF NONBEING

On the other side of Sinai
an uncommanded poet
who never was in Egypt
a desert passerby, who glances up,
disturbed by lightning in a rainless sky,
the sounds of ram horns tearing open thought
and hears, "I am the Lord"
and as a poet
sees colors that will never have a name,
the colors of unbeing God becoming.

LAST EVENING, I WATCH THE GARDEN SWALLOW MY FRIENDS

Guests sit in teakwood chairs and a sofa
outside, men talk of poetry
the white thighs of women show
toes pointing at pink roses
the scent of flowers sweetens all ideas
invisibly, irresistibly.
A yellow dragon watches from under the hibiscus
stretches, scales still glittering
as the sun fades, wings folded
as if at peace.

Late Winter after the Election

The vine shoots trail on red soil
like our banners after
the saddening strife
we rue our losses, but rain will fall
and new tendrils hidden in the forest
already rise and leaves unfurl like flags.

MOUNTAINS AND RIVERS

Settling into vast landscapes and mindscapes
trying to prove congruency
hierarchies of green-white branches
rising to the tiny sunbirds' trills
his flashing, gleaming neon
perhaps improving the heavens' blues
until the mind is vacant but alert
and the watcher reaches out
a hand, banked stream of blood
and the soaring, unscalable mind
refracting colors, before we turn to words.

"Rivers and mountains" refers to a genre of Chinese poetry. This poem will, I
hope, make more sense in the context of some other poems on the general theme.

On my Seventy-ninth Birthday I Examine my Zoological Garden

with Particular Attention to Recent (Last Decade) Additions

I pull my fingers quickly back
from the carnivorous koalas
munching eucalyptus leaves, a salad
before the main course, and in their caves
the dragons, the yellow beast who rubs
his scaly snout on my outstretched hand
wings neatly folded, fires off,
and the hissing, sneering white scaled serpent
whose stare, as much as his unbanked flame
embodies evil, and in warm ashes singing
is the phoenix, her aerie vast as mind
and overhead, black and a rain-glossed green,
the secret dragons circling the moon
no cage can hold. The rows go on, until I see myself
staring back, this cage a mirror
more accurate than any glass.

READING K'ANG YOUWEI (1858-1927)

"Therefore if man cuts off the substance of love which is the
mind that cannot bear to see the suffering of others, moral
principles of mankind will be destroyed and terminated.
If these are destroyed and terminated, civilization will
stop and mankind will revert to barbarism. Furthermore,
barbarism will stop and men will revert to their original
animal nature."

We are at stage three, barbarism.
Twenty-six Afghans died today
in a suicide bombing. Eighteen children in Yemen
starved next door to a harbor piled in wheat
because we can bear the suffering of others.
In Tel Aviv I have seen women search for food
through supermarket garbage, and we killed thirty
people in Gaza who were trying to kill me.
A green lizard scampers up a stucco wall
under a white rose vine. My cat watches murderous
full of the animal nature she has never left.
The gray cat, the green vine and lizard,
a different, darker green, and
the white flowers, the garden's soul
and I call the cat, I can't bear
to see the suffering of others. That
is the substance of love.

Reading Li Bai in the Garden

The shadow of a white butterfly
floats over the white rose
floats over the page in my book
beats both wings down then up
no longer a shadow, a force in the world,
hurricane maker in Florida
or generating snow in Siberia.
The shadow of a white butterfly floats
over the page and suddenly a poem appears,
just this poem, ten lines, like fingers.

RESPONSE TO THE FLOWERS SUSANN CUT, ARRANGED IN A VASE, AND PLACED IN FRONT OF A TRIPLE MIRROR ON HER DRESSER IN OUR BEDROOM

I am reading the I-Ching.
Out of the yin earth of garden soil
drawn by the yang of sun and recent rain
into this world of the ten thousand things
multiplied by mirrors so that four
images of beauty fill the room I lie in
and one of these is real, scent-full,
making me conscious of creation's soul
and three are simulacra
were I a bee, three would disappear
perhaps, be drawn to the other glass
where snapdragons flower twice.

SUNBIRDS REPLY TO THE HUANGLONG

Huanglong, the yellow scholar dragon
whispers behind white waving Stippa grass
in the light green breeze that forms
inside our gray stone garden walls.
she slithers over Phoenix ash to tell
of chariots and gods and what is coming,
of resurrections and recurrence
blossoming and the interims of being.
Above, the sunbirds flash their bright blue feathers
insisting, singing now and now and now
here on this branch, hear now and now and now.

THE PAGE OF WINTER TURNS AND SPRING APPEARS

I sit before my winter garden
ending now as spring
with brazen yellow dragon claws
tears open hard coiled buds
so red and orange flowers on the low nasturtiums
surround and glow against the rising callas.
I'm granted yet another spring
my seventy-ninth awakening
by the gracious God of seasons
and in my heart-mind
the memory of youth is youth again.

The Way in our Garden

1

The Way splits soil between the jasmine
not in flower now, early March
and the orange-berried Duranta, deep green leaved
not shining like the jasmine's
but feeding bulbuls and other singing visitors
and then the Way bends right into deep shade
runs miles and miles unseen until it breaks
back into sight a thousand miles away
where Belamcanda fiercely raises spears
against the Tartar weeds. I see the Way
go further, disappear, in age and green,
all time and space, and an acacia,
tall tree over the garden wall.

2

The Way divides in paving slabs and tracks
barely wide enough for hopping palm doves
and not bound by black soil
in flyways over pink sage into white-leaved trees
perhaps the Way sinks underneath blue Trachelium
where worms and moles live out their karma.
Sometimes the Way because all Ways are one
crashes into the cold gray outer stones
the impassable garden's end.

3

The Way runs right today
behind the varicolored annuals
aglow like road signs in some Daoist sky
and through blue pansies, white alyssum clumped
aims at the olive tree and bright blue birds
before it veers at almond tree's white blossoms
a crossroad where Elaine stands beautiful
at a square in Greenwich Village
holding my hand and laughing, it is noon
her red hair shines near the naked fig tree
and I hold the box of food we've bought to take
to her home on Seventh Street, underneath the lime tree
while in Sweden, near the loquat tree, Susann is four years old
waiting for me and growing, growing
unknown, lighting the Way.

4

I face right across the paved driveway limping
I use my walking stick, black metal,
I step where weeds emerge behind the red concrete
with Susann's arm for balance and clear sight
of a weedy lot we cross, stopping and stepping slow
across a rare and weedy flowering forever afternoon
bending to see the tiny yellow flowers
bursting from the dark nothingness of time
into our always space, a place the Way
circles and we have now and now is always —
a vacant lot, infinite in size, green and still wet with spring
wild flower blue and yellow
a place lovers can show each other now and then
a place for talking, a place to speak with love
the Way lost in the distance.

5

The Way is women always
my Mother a red geranium despite her wish
for leafy green, a five year old who knew a red blossom
but couldn't see root, stem, and leaf
that border my garden Way now
and all the Susann years in Pardesiya.
My Father's Mother a fig tree in the Bronx
bent earthward wrapped in winter
a time-bend in my Way where now and now
a fig tree decorates its winter limbs
with leaf buds, twelve feet high, unbound.

6

Karen's bra yellow as buttercup
when she surprised me undressing
a byway too beautiful a dragon beware
I think of her now in warm winter
a Way not taken, a path glowing
in a different garden.

7

A stone wall blocks the Way
I turn aside and seek a green path back
but even butterflies can stutter over
and bulbuls, sparrows, sunbirds
palm doves and on top chameleons
bask and run zigzag over up and down.
Moles and earthworms tunnel mouth stuffed dirt
making their Ways and giggling past me.

8

Letters arrive from friends I'll never see
to show the lupines, whiter now than purple
flowering where the Way approaches home
by the concrete stairs and black scarred wooden door
the smell of herbs, the new Breynia
escaped from where the patio ends
and also end this foreign English meter.
Upstairs again, I try to write replies
across far skies and oceans.

9

The Way winds right behind a rock
where fruitless strawberries sprawl
and then divides in time
one track almost straight up where Father sits
a hand caressing Mother and a track
turns down, I lie on my dead Grandfather's bed
in the Bronx, naked, with a girl I've more than met
and towards the wall, crashing, with Elaine
talking of Donne's sonnets, making love
before the Way converges in a rise of columbines.

10

The Way this winter stays its chilling course
under the loquat tree that swells with fruit
as if it were spring, and the lime tree's blossom buds
echo, their perfume tensely coiled
as pure erotic, looking for release
as fig leaves shape already cover
for modesty. Spontaneous creation
out of winter formlessness, and memory stops
unneeded in spring's gathering now.

Three Butterflies

Sun simmers the tall yellow flowers
of the Senna, climbing the unresisting palm.
Wet heat — the drops of sweat containing each
distillate of dragon breath
and the red Pentas wave flags of rebellion
no flower has the energy to engage
and only two white butterflies
dying anyway, poke antennae forward, eager
as any old man to live the parting days
fully, hot, tired, looking for some cool shade.

WAKING DRAGONS: AFTER THE ISRAELI ELECTION

Late winter greets this early spring
with an unfurling calla lily
and black-faced yellow pansies
repeat, Bill Wordsworth
writes, and underneath two dragons
stretch and stir in Loki's graveyard
their wet wings look for air. From every
radio and new delivered newspaper
white evil dragons snarl, and crouched afraid
my yellow dragon friend recoils.

We Search for Li on the Patio

We sit with friends from far away
looking at the springtime garden
the leaves of the tall shrubs return now
from the depths of winter, white flowers
again cover the ground. The pattern of the season
is the pattern of old friendships.

"Li" has multiple meanings, one of which "correct customary behavior."

WINTER IN ISRAEL

Green sog clots deep mud
olive-jade dragon scales cover earth now
thorny weeds thrust to heaven
red rose persists, yang in a woman's world
four days of rain, dark winter wet
ends Phoenix fires
oozy black ash. Dark thoughts.

Yellow Flowers: A Daoist Dreamvision

A yellow trumpet flower hangs near the iron gate
from Paratrooper Road into the garden
the poison flower guards, the smallest taste
engenders visions of another world
a Dao Eden, a place of immortals
riding cranes, the long necks stretched out
towards islands of the blessed. A second taste
is death, beneath the yellow flowers
in the heavy midnight scent, intoxicating
as bottles of good wine and better verse
lie bodies. Many bodies.
On Paratrooper Road tanks ride by on carriers.

Spring May Have Arrived

I sit on the paved patio in the sun
a weed vine skirts the multihued Breynia
and in an axil flirts a single flower
small as an idea, pure purple
beautiful as the dress a girl once wore
holding my arm, smiling, at seventeen
and I was seventeen too, smiling
and I see the broad while fragrant calla lily
weddings and funerals
and a red rose for her corsage
to make myself seventeen again.

The New Year: 5779

A sunbird weaves and darts
between white butterflies
feeding on the blue hibiscus —
a sapphire tossed into snow
rapidly falling on still water.
The hot autumn sun
freezes and melts.
This year I shall be seventy-nine
watching the great changes.

Falling in the Autumn Garden

On my buttocks, splayed weak legs point out
unable to rise, my back useless here
on the hard patio cement and granite tiles
ranunculus wakes up in its clay pots
calla lilies force through the nasturtium
flowering orange and red at my curled toes
bees sleep in their hives birds peck.
My wife helps me stand again
a few buds show on rose bushes.

I Was Born in 1940, a Year of the Dragon

This year I wash the scales, still mossy green,
with desalinated water from
the Mediterranean Sea, and comb cobwebs
from thinning, velvety wings,
sharpen teeth on rocks dredged up from sea bottom,
yellowed fangs scraping gray-green stones.
A dragon lives as long
as who he guards
with sharp fire red, the blue-white core
less than it was. He takes up space,
a beast who rarely flies who soared once,
shutting out the moon, a glorious cloud.
It is hard work, this dragon care.

Necessity

Hui Shi, Prime Minister of Wei, ordering his armies
against Qin, wrote war as impossible as
two-headed cranes, deciding where to fly
and where to nest. His friend Zhuangzi
arranged a mirror so one crane head
disappeared. Zhuangzi laughed.
Hui Shi removed all hollows, left alone
one nesting place. The Dao was one,
Hsing-er-shang fused in ch'i,
or form in matter.
Zhuangzi repaired to study, while Hui Shi
ordered his troops to battle.

THE WORLD UNDER HEAVEN

A breeze dances the white Stippa grass
to a low cloud and early rain
stripped the poisonous beautiful yellow
Datura of most leaves. Sunbirds dart
between white butterflies.
From the synagogue down the street
a man blows a ram horn trumpet
so a rhythm surrounds
and orders this existence.

Indoors

Green fig leaves, tall grass plumes red and waving
in a wind I cannot feel here
and orange flowers from a neighbor's vine
against a low stone wall.
Perhaps there are sweet scents
and the passing of butterflies.
I have only a window
and piles of books where
sometimes a dragon lurches
snorting fire and truth.

First Jottings of the New Year

Black pigeon's blacker after rain
wet feathers and an orange beak.
a light brown pigeon also perches
on my windowsill. Behind
a red tile roof higher than
the young mango tree. It has not rained.
Li-Young Lee calls me to his poem,
"Ceremony of the Intended"
so I can spend a little time
breathing outside of time.

I STEP OUTSIDE INTO THE GARDEN AND

I count twenty of the thousand greens
sixteen of the thousand browns
fourteen purples and my eyes close
mindful of colors, my nose scents four sweetnesses
and my fingers feel twelve sharpnesses of leaf edge
all in the first twelve feet
between the glass door and the first rose bush.
This means nothing but all meaning is here,
if I place this jar down as a center.

Homeland, Soulland

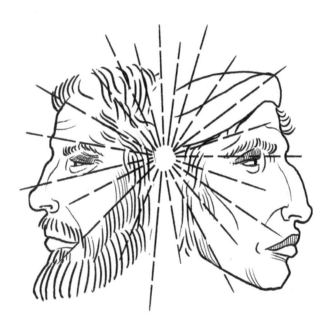

ALEXANDER THE GREAT

*who died June 10, 323 BCE, and marched south through
Pardesiya*

Alexander the Great shuffles through the sand
twelve feet under my topsoil, half asleep
from trudging south, or swaying
left to right to left on horseback, dreams
of a feast in Damascus, girls and boys,
a lot of local wine, and now to Egypt,
blood, loot, and after that the order
and the new city with his name. Here
is passage, a dry and narrow way. Coast
birds scraw and skee above. No hint
of us, our tons of soil and water,
the roses, law courts, streets
laid out so logically, athletic fields,
we might as well speak Greek, perhaps
you rested here, spoke to the natives, us.

And Isaac Was Comforted After the Death of his Mother

Genesis 24:67

Each leaf stood stark
the car whirred down
the empty highway in
a tunnel, glassed panels, frames
of grass and trees, locked
snapshots that I don't
know how to throw away
in dreams and sometimes waking.
Seventy miles an hour
for sixteen years so far.
The hearse is far in front
my hands (a friend is driving)
are one along a thigh the other
stroking a breast. I do not cry
I do not love the girl
I'm grateful to
and can't remember her
except her name, only the trees
in spring,
in April underwear
of crisp light green,
oak, maple, sassafras and elm
against a green-gray sky.
Father was dead all day
and I

wanted to get laid, and did
that night, the funeral
hurting to ice, the dark
hiding that I spewed tears
deep in that sympathy.

BE FRUITFUL AND MULTIPLY

A Midrash

A better version: "Blossom and increase."
But still, Rabbi, inadequate. Blossom.
Yes, the grass, the mosses in their way,
cockroach and hummingbird, the spiders
in my corner, running back and forth
between ground and the ceiling, bloom
in their time, flower beyond reason.

The desert dense with waiting seed
and seed alive underneath glaciers.
Seed has survived in pyramids,
the oceans are full of seed —
spawn, spore and sperm,
male and female seed —
some seed never dies
excepting fire, and maybe stars are seed.

A person or a flower in each piece,
abstract of sprout, shadow of increase,
the iris tip a swollen leaf
until it color a week, unroll
like a woman easing down her blanket;
then the purple, and feather yellow
opens like truth, like honey —
the single mouth with nine tongues.

"Which is more real, the mouth or what it says?"
This flower shouts its presence grandly.
"Does seed give bloom more than a brief few days?"
Yes, listen Rabbi: blossom and be many.

Beer Sheva: Various Occasions

I. An Evening

Fringed fronds stretch
longer, then taller,
until they touch, higher,
than clouds, and green
black implications
reveal themselves
Through the darkening gray;
my neighbor's daughter
moves with her friend
under the streetlight
for the night's last kiss.

II. Howling

The infant screams against the wind
in cold and hunger, the desert storms to fill
a different emptiness, and the hounds howl,
afraid of what that is; only the jackals
lie quiet in holes under wet stones —
tonight side channels of the *wadi*
will arrange jackal tracks like tracery
and cubs feast full in the moon's flood.

BOMBING GAZA: DEAD CHILDREN

I am in favor, madam, of bombing you
and yours, how not a poem that is, a child
in pieces, blood and severed limbs
and scattered teeth and bones, her mother, you,
holding up a torso, sobbing, hating
me and all the Jews who send the planes
that kill you and your kind. I will not cry
your tears. Beneath the ruin and rocks
that were your world are men who try to kill
my daughter, grandson, all that matters
more to me than you, so you and yours
are in my way. This is no poem, madam,
and it will never be. Just one of us
will rise tomorrow, grimly and so sad.

A JUGGLE OF MYRTLE TWIGS

They tell of R. Judah b. R. Ila'i that he used to take a myrtle
twig and dance before the bride and say: 'Beautiful and
graceful bride.' R. Samuel b. R. Issac danced with three
twigs. ....When he died, a pillar of fire came between him
and the whole of the rest of the world.

Ketubot 17a

To stop time, a twig spinning
always on top, two side sprigs,
a trick of the eye, the eyes
of the groom and bride, a wall of fire
between R. Samuel and the other just
of his generation. Myrtle for its smell
to fix time in the mind, the dance
so time, stopped by illusion,
moved with art and sensually
in the Rabbi's feet, in the close
three bunched myrtle leaves, the three sticks
turning and tumbling, only a rustle
revealed their turning and tumbling.
The bride was led away by ladies
before R. Samuel's strength softened,
the small branches slowing
speeded time to what, in his own end
was a great fire: the honor comes
only once or twice in an age.

Tonight, no juggler, unable
to offer prestidigitation

against clocks or calendars
or to compete with odors
of the bride, the countryside,
here, in late March, I mix
words for you, that won't stay still
themselves, be more than memory,
but I know love held R. Samuel
out of time and moving while he had strength, and you
know that all that love can do.

CETERO CENSEUM GAZANEN
ESSE DELENDA

They never will abate these seventy years
of unremitting hate, never speak peace
and mean it, decrease the will to extirpate
the Jewish State that, ever more powerful,
is a barbed arrow in the pride, the hard neck
behind the Arab throat. Ten thousand pages,
weeks and months of argument across
television screens and not one mind
changed, even disturbed by rhetoric
practiced by masters. No one is listening,
no one cares, like bears discussing a hunting ground
or even plants, groping for sun.
Maybe a new city, an Arab Cartagena
or a Mediterranean Singapore
will come next but this, an afternoon
spent deeply sheltered, not even hating
those so sworn to hate they choose to die
has got to stop.

COMING HOME: BEER SHEVA

On top the heap is sand and yellow stone.
The *tel* side slopes away into the *wadi*
whose waters trapped in winter kept alive
our long, long dead. From the modern city
we visit diggings, see how heavy rock
barriers we built still keep their shape, gray
casemate and, below the burned level, darker
solid blocks. Rough shards and silver coins
are on display and the highly glazed
fragments of pots and multicolored glass
made beautiful by fire in the second
burned level down. Deeper it isn't us
and no one mourns the children's bones interred
in cornerstones, offerings to some god
forgotten, annihilated in the fire we made
establishing the third burned level down.
And it goes on through further towns and fires
that interest not even ghosts. In the valley
where we live, eyes flame, coins and dishes drop.

EASTER 1969

It didn't work. That much
is obvious. Your nails were
unrusted before the next murder,
and outside your grave
there was some jostling
for position. The long term
effects have actually been worse.
(Though to be fair,
tortures and dismemberments in your name
would probably have been done
in someone else's.) By the time
your boards warped, you were words
and in the clutch of critics.

EASTER 2021

We are already always redeemed
salvation cut into our penises
God's love carved in us
like initials of high school sweethearts
in a schoolyard oak. Is this the future
of my first line, the one about redemption,
or is it still the present of this poem?
Should a future with an axe approach
to chop down the lovers' oak the lovers
stay timelessly in God and named there.

Epithalamion

For the marriage of Ethel and Patrizia
Jaffa, May 2019

The usual citrus scents of Israeli spring
songbirds trying to settle in fruit trees
bothered by our bagpipes, twitters awry
as my old friend gets married tonight
to a woman she loves. Two gray-haired ladies
heavy in their age, pledge troth and press their souls
together. A muezzin's evening screed is holy text
enough for the gathering. I know Holy
whenever I luck upon it. I thank you.

FATHERS AND SONS

A father's guilt is this: that
aging Abraham heard the voice
of our dementing God and did not
hesitate but, in release,
later, twisted the knife that killed
the tangled ram. It was not
only one animal that died that day.

And it is this, too: that
we have heard the game oracle
that filled the Theban's head
with blood and blackness:

The father is redeemed, a son
is unforgiven for a father
and must be destroyed, perhaps to live
in a new way, with new eyes.

For Yehuda Halevi

My heart's in the highlands
my heart is not here

or

my heart is in the East
but my mind, wallet
and general sense of self
are all in a house near Boston
where I plan to leave them

or

I spent sixteen years in Israel
paid the taxes
wore the uniform
felt the fronds sway in a wind I owned
dug sowed reaped
voted
and laughing left and thanked God I had;
kissed the tarmac at Kennedy.

I read *Ma'ariv* weekends and *Ha'aretz* every day
Still longin' for the old plantation
glad that I'm far far away.

Yehuda Halevi was a major Jewish-Spanish poet of the middle ages. He wrote poems of longing for Zion, the most famous of which begins "…My heart is in the east and I in the far west." *Ma'ariv* and *Ha'aretz* are Israeli daily newspapers.

GOD CALLS THE STARS BY NAME

For the New Jewish High School's Astronomy Day
January 24, 2001

> *He counts out the number of the stars*
> *And gives each one of them a name.*
>
> Psalms 147:4

We have no constellations
because we have no gods.
Samson pursues no lion and no hair
falls shorn through space.
No Pharaoh's army plunges axle deep
in stars banked up
in muddy milky ways.

And each star has a name we do not know
in God talk. Perhaps we too.

Do you arrange the sky that is arranged
beyond imagining? There are no dotted lines
outside the myth of mind
where gods and bears and stars we have misnamed
split heaven.

We name our children
and we name ourselves
draw lines around us
and we live in them
and try to shine.

I Understand Too

*Hamas has understood what the ideology of terror has
clearly espoused for over a hundred years. When attacking
a democracy, the terrorist has to put it in a quandary.
The way to do that is to force the democracy to kill civil-
ians. So if you set up your terror-base under a school or
a hospital, you've got it made in the shade. You launch
missiles, for example, against Israel. Now the Israelis have
a choice. Either they don't respond, in which case the
terror mounts in the face of ongoing impotence, or they
do respond, in which case you're going to have civilian
deaths and dramatic pictures for the West's nightly news.*

Simcha Jacobovici, *Times of Israel*,
July 28, 2014

The color photo of the little girl
maybe eight years old, it's hard to tell
for half her head is missing, been blown off,
not cropped by Photoshop, and though I don't
applaud, I do accept that shit does really
happen, disturbs me. I'm in a quandary.
I must accept your right to blow the heads
off little Jewish girls or send the bombs
to kill that little Arab girl. It's like
those problems we drank beers over, after
ethics class, but with real people so it's
more interesting, it counts, as I count
syllables and note the music of my
lines. No name is given in the news report

about the little Arab girl, and that
is bad, I'd name her in a prayer
but not apology, that wouldn't make
the news, apology in vain like all the rest.

Rain Falls Hard on the Spring Garden, and Other News Arrives

Last night black dragons fought loudly overhead
we heard them thundering and this morning
a bomb awoke us, sirens warning
of white dragons gathering in the south
wet Gaura leaves pushed up as spears
and my son presents us with a grandchild.

HER PARENTS HAIRY

For Ariel Nehama

Her parents hairy with unswollen breasts
hold hands against her. Women she does not know
lift and unwrap her. Pallas Athena
ripped wholly and entire from two heads.

My friends embrace the child they have conceived,
imagined baby, immaculate in mind
formed female flesh and knowledged in the folds
of fertile skin. Engendered Ariel.

Comforting lion of God, Athena,
Alethea: how shall we bless you here?
Be fruitful like your mothers Sarah, Rivka,
Rachel and Leah, baby born in mind
and carried in hard arms. So much condensed
of mores in a crib and in these lines!
Learn love from hairy fathers, Ariel,
and swell to womanhood.

"Comforting lion of God" is a loose translation of Ariel Nehama.

Indeed, a Great Share

Re'em al-Reyashi, a Palestinian mother of two who killed two Israelis in a suicide bombing Wednesday, professed love for her children before launching an attack that said was meant to turn her body into "deadly shrapnel."

Reuters, Gaza, January 15, 2004

Re'em, I also want to soar
free of the mortal, to penetrate
as man the softest parts and portals.

"I always wanted to be the first woman
to carry out a martyr attack where parts of my body
can fly all over," she said, smiling.
"That is the only wish I can ask God for."

Re'em in love completely, making love
to her four men. Their blood and bodies fused
like God and God.

Her children rise and bless Re'em.
Her husband praises her.
For each lover her soul sings:
"Your heart is pierced
several times so that I penetrate
to your entrails. When I draw me out, you think
I am drawing them out with me
and you leave me completely
afire with a great love of God."

Those who dispatched you, Re'em,
hate your woman's body
like pig flesh, like the uncircumcised,
like Zionists. They broke it and rendered.
But you were love, Re'em,
and in last song you cried:

"So excessive was the sweetness
caused by this intense pain
that I could never wish to lose it, nor would my soul
be content with anything less.
It is not bodily pain, but spiritual,
though the body has a share in it —
indeed, a great share."

Some of the lines attributed to Re'em al-Reyashi were written by St. Theresa of
Avila.

Guarding the Primary School
(Beer Sheva, Israel, 1978)

We walk slowly through the mud inside
the barbed wire fences looking for explosives
or signs of strangers. In the shaggy
child-mauled shrubbery I discover spring
in the holes dug around the pines
to hold water full now yellow flowers burst
on the piled dirt ridges half-inch high
violets prepare themselves for their time soon
in clumps along the spiked barrier.
The children sing *shaharit;* the birds
parcel the schoolyard inspect tree tops
and school-house eaves in sexier song.
Outside the water flows down desert
followed by sheep black goats black-robed
Bedouin women red embroidered
loosely veiled soaking the desert
dandelion clover high grasses. Guns shift
uneasily unnecessarily till they pass.
The death outside. We keep the death outside.

JUST WAR

Ashrei yanks on my beard, both hands
and it hurts, really, I ouch and the year old
grandson chortles. In Gaza, a ten
year old boy falls to pieces, a bomb
meant for someone else, I guess,
booms him to death. I write
that the bomb had to fall. I mean it,
I have to mean it. I mean it.

MY HOLY NAME

I fantasized a saint, a scholar rabbi
flustered from his learning — a Salanter,
a Haim of Volozhin leaning down
from Talmud towards a lost and sobbing child,
dowering brides anonymously
black clad and clean, humble and hungry. No.

In Ramat Gan, a linguist, genealogist,
smiling above his gin and tonic, told me
Codish, holy, was a martyr's name,
granted an ancestor slower than a Cossack,
sliced down and trampled under horse's hooves
so leaving us his children his new name.

It wasn't hard to get used to — the suddenness,
the certainty, and knowing my last name.
I never doubted. Easier for me then
to imagine abject fear than piety.

Weaving through slushy snow after his futile
flight, my two times great-grandfather read
the glittering blade edge skittering towards him,
writing in blue gray sky a sidewise stroke,
a downward slash, and another — deeper -
the arm raised up again and balanced slowly,
again the earthward thrust, a curse, a third
missed stroke and finally a whirl above
his head, the last triumphant swirl and bite

of steel in flesh. *Koph, vav, dalet, shin,*
accurate letters on always alien air —
the script of blood and iron named me holy.

Poem at Sixty-two

When God created the world He consulted the Torah.
The Torah was written in black fire on white fire.

Midrash Tanhuma

God was young then.

There was white paper, foolscap or snow
for scribbling or staring, black or bird tracked
readable close up or from the window
upstairs, closed always in terminable winter
or bond with linen, later a white screen
blue script and pixels. (It is spring. Pink
cherry flame and yellows burn my eyes.)
Then I wrote gray on gray
hiding. Love or hate could read
and taste wrong, like orange meat
or chrome potatoes. Writing confusion so
confusing reading.

Now I write clearly
(or more nearly clear) on pages almost night
as darkness smiles its welcome. I scrape away
the ink or soot or ash paper becomes now
without my ministrations. Vision also fades
but not the mind. This poem is translated
(and so is wrong or else a different right)
from white on black, back to black on white.

The world to come is written entirely in
black fire on black fire.

PURIM 5779

Lilacs grew first in Persia
and Persian women long ago knew
that peaches and apricots sweeten chicken
sautéed in butter, spiced
with cinnamon and dark cloves
served at the ancient royal festivities
where Vashti lost her crown
and Jewish Esther, beautiful
as the purple flowers scenting
the king's table, sat afterwards
sad in her mission, our anointed queen.

In a Small Clearing of Time
in the Jungle of Years

Our forest has just six trees
lining our one house village
in a country of four people
two of them in splendid residence
and there are travelers passing through
not counting the immortals riding cranes
and the immensities of myth
the history, the four thousand years.

TEACHING HEBREW

I'm not and never was a Hebrew teacher
but when Geveret Mandelstein took ill
I filled in. Nine teenage students sat
bewildered at the strange Semitic squiggles,
the ancient grammar of their father tongue.

Learning their own language at fourteen —
wolf children cub-napped from the comfort woods,
smooth words their mothers crooned them into this
guttural ancient desert, a memory-
world where even memory is created —
makes them howl. But until this they lived
in a world strangers translated, kindly
or not. We cover nakedness; these Jews
become themselves, fluent and at home.

The Arab Question

The Arab Question
is unpayable bills, long silences
in a too long marriage kept
for the children's sake, and
other embarrassments.

Remember how you shivered as a child
reading of Secret Police
and Slavery and the delicious horrors
the Cossacks, Huns, Mongols and whoever
committed — and wondered aloud
how ever anyone could act like that
but knew inside exactly how they could.

The tabloid and the radio tell us all
about an Arab father buggering
his three year old son. On the street,
waiting for the bus, heads nod knowingly.

Maybe one morning we'll wake up
and they'll all be gone. Maybe
the neighbor's daughter stares at me
lovesick and horny.

I grew up in Camden, New Jersey, myself.
The Negroes lived far away,
went to other schools,
cleaned the streets,

ate different food, and
had weird sexual habits.
They all carried knives.

I'm afraid of them, too,
walking alone in the Old City of Jerusalem,
away from the crowds.

In Gaza once, on reserve duty,
I talked to the old gardener at the fort
about roses and hollyhocks
and then searched his pockets
and the lunch bag on his bicycle
and ran my hands under his arms
and between his legs.

It's not that America is better than here
but there it's not our fault.

This is a very nasty poem. I wrote it in Petah Tikva, Israel, in 1987. It explains, in part, why we left Israel, although not permanently.

Back in Israel

A hoopoe stands in my yard
pecking in the dirt
and I think of him, and that he is not
a kosher bird, according to Leviticus,
which calls him a "dooqyfat."
(I wasn't going to eat him anyway,
but suddenly he mattered.)
Everything — or almost — matters here
and that can crush thought
especially when you are young
and everything already matters
sometimes too much, and in both
my mother tongue and my father tongue.

for long connections
with misremembered pasts golden and singing,
for kings and poets who can no more exist
than the God who makes hoopoes from earth
or men and women from memorial dust —
the God I love and pray to —
renew our days as of old.

and in wings barred black and white.
If it is a hoopoe,
my sandals cut into my toes
and I am an old poet half blind
planning my last garden,
looking for my last dog.

May I be as misremembered as my God,
as powerless and beloved.
The garden will bloom; a puppy
romp, chasing birds.

Good Friday

It didn't work. That much is obvious.
Before your boards warped you were words
and in the impious hands of critics.
After the misery of all these years.
I grant your awful pain, but still I saw
my grandfather die more slowly and still more
painfully from lung cancer, and my cousin
Johnny cough his twenty years out in six months
with no great Father hope to ease the end.
Still, what if you believed this was for us?
The rest, your revolutionary good crowd
want us to die for them, sometimes we do
like singing Judas sheep, the last march through.

NEW YEAR 5739

The apple dipped in honey shows the snake
who whispered through his funny fangs at Eve
was honest about ends although his means
lacked, what Adam couldn't hope for, humanness,
and anyway the tree was not the tree
three sinners thought, thrown out for childish hope,
not act, for a naive belief in magic fruit
that bored God mad with silly he and she
who pass the bowl tonight, no smarter now
than all those thousand years ago. The snake
grown old and tired, piles gold skins and red
in heaps we use to pay the bill we got.
He watches us crunch wishes in our teeth
and wonders what went wrong that we went right.

THE BURNING OF NOTRE DAME, 2019

For gargoyles, today is the uncarving,
is Independence Day, the day the grinning grim
and pestilent skulls tear free in red hot ash
and pour on Paris, and not only there
but all of cursed Christendom in its beauty
of stone and colored glass enshrined
millennia of Jew hate, women tied
to slavery of sex while Christian armies
marched blessed by priests. We
gargoyles falling sing our Ave Maria
in raspy happy rubbing, growling stone.

THE MAN FROM AUSCHWITZ

The man from Auschwitz killed my daughter's cat.
The ugly Jew with twisted tattooed hands
spread poison on the grass and her kitten died
on the neighbor's walk, a soft gray mass of fluff
my daughter loved and spoke her first words to,
said kittycat before she burbled daddy.
The spiteful Jew who lives next door and dreams
of death and gas and choking killed her cat
and watched the little beast writhe morning out
looking at his dead wife and three dead sons
in old gilt picture frames, and the old man smiled —
the crazy Jew I hate who lives next door
and the Germans, and all Christian Europe
who poisoned Minnie, Idit's little cat.

The Most Important Divine Commandment Is "Choose Life!"

At the front door a stone urn holds
purple verbena, and then sharp Gaura spears
deep pink as fresh blood, and further
grass spikes, yellow Senna, pink Antigone vine
climbing fences, the palm tree, the green-gray olive tree
all leading to the iron gate
mezuzah marked as entrance, exit,
while soldiers ordered to our living space
from the US, Iran, Turkey, Russia,
and by every terrorist captain
try to convince me that these colors,
scents, Susann's loving work here,
all the choices of life
matter less than these gathering heaps of death.

THE RAIN

In mid-November storm and lightning blazed
a power pole, the dog whined, rain blessed
or over-blessed the winter garden. There
are winter flowers, soaked and fragrant still.
Na'el al-Kordi is dead, waiting to enter
Israel for cancer treatment. I hope
the rain waited with him near Gaza.
Last night I walked my dog through puddles,
deeper than paws, under bright lights
patrolled, sometimes, on Paratrooper Road,
and came in through the dormant shrubs.
We ate chicken Florentine, pasta
with a mushroom sauce, and drank Riesling.
Every drop matters here, this seven month long
desert, wine and water. Late at night, sometimes,
planes fly low. This is not an easy place
to live, but it is very beautiful.
Na'el died in his mother's arms.
He was a terrorist, the army said.
This morning, I slipped on a soapy floor,
I fell and broke a toe. The clinic wants me
to get X-rays. It is raining again,
the anemones will flourish, and so
shall we, or many of us, writing,
growing flowers, eating well, nervous.

THEOLOGIAN

When students ask me about God
and they do, leaning at my table at lunch
elbows propped on the pecan parquetry
or sprawled backwards on the caned chairs,
school gossip over and the roast veal eaten,
our wine drunk, the salads nibbled,
the world's bounty cleared and put away —
Saturday afternoon, God means but isn't,
I say and I explain.

They speak.

Once books fell — history, philosophy, religion —
and curses scoured until they both
reshelved them. Then they tore
each other's hearts out leaving those
to stain the carpeted floor.
"I don't trust books," she said,
"they just don't help."

His sister furtives out before lunch.
He is glad. In class, she dreamed of Amsterdam
and dope, went dumpster diving in Oakland.

Of God who isn't I speak, and how God means.
My son's poems are being published.
He has been straight for weeks, I think,
four months out of the hospital,

and understands God talk. Susann has heard
God talk before. She worries about me.

Well, there is no God and we obey Him,
our food kosher, the Sabbath's laws observed
exactly. We welcome guests
always and well. Books line the walls —
poetry, theology, history, philosophy, drama —
and the carpets lie thick and undisturbed.

On all our faces just a smear of God.

The Riots in Palestine

In mid-winter, Rivka's great mango tree
approaches flower and the small Arabs
are dead, uncurling fingers around rocks.
And it is luck or lot if the ruddy
yellow fruit will form this year (last year
three mangos from a great old tree) or if
the young Arabs, boys and girls, will fall
unripe and hard. Rivka knows this, and the Arabs,
and the soldiers shooting.
        The *jinni* knew this,
all the old gods knew this, the *baalim*,
the demons in their groves and among the hills
and the spirits in the stones and stunted trees.
The Lord and Allah are grown pale and gaunt.
Iblis and Azazel gnaw their lambs and taunt.

VICTORY!

"We won," said Hamas leader Ismail Haniyeh in his first
statement since the ceasefire on Tuesday.
Ynet News, August 5, 2014

Enjoy and celebrate, Ismail Haniyeh,
ankle deep at least in Arab blood
in the flowerless *souks* of Gaza. Wave
flags and baby bodies side by side
and sell tickets to the next game.

Tear down the goal posts, winner, try
to stand up in the ruins, concrete blocks
and shattered, twisted steel. We losers
wish you well, and in real pity
wish you may win no more. Here
flowers grow, our houses flourish too
and gladly we accept defeat.

I Remember a Northern Garden While I Am Home in Israel

There was wisdom in the winter garden
white twigs on rime frost ground
memories of snow and icicles
even in this suburb of Eden
but the yellow green of spring
red poppies just too bright to be believed
has its wisdom too and I a white haired man
staring out a window, wishing I was a sage.

IN THE GARDEN, JUNE 2019

Moss rose gems sprinkled glowing
in front of the roses, red now,
and pink and russet Breynia leaves
in the near right garden side
purple and green leaves of the treelike
eight foot tall Australian shrub
in front of the white stone wall.
Beyond it the street and the mental hospital
where guards patrol the mowed grass
and ambulances sometimes wail their sirens
to the screech of brakes and parakeets
screech too, feral escapees, safe now
in the tall surrounding eucalyptus trees.

I Have Learned

to keep myself apart
somewhat from flesh
which vanishes but
I am unlearning,. I
am in love again, the perishing
oil and wine and what
cannot be named
refill my stores.

Paranoia in a Spring Garden

Among the flowering shrubs of May
stitched together by spiders
full of birds singing in strange tongues
suffused with scents of the season
pink flowers on low sage plants
the color deepening and adding red and blue
in the Leucoforms and climbing
to the deep blue of the Duranta
my eyes find a deep cove, a mind cave
I hurry into. Now I am safe
I do not know from what.

A Palm Dove 2014: Wartime

Outside the bathroom window, on a stone
faced ledge, alone and silent in the sun
at noon, a palm dove, purple deep, a sign
of peace like her white friends, but rarer yet.
Her home is near the top, hidden in long leaves
of our date palm, male, unbearing, clothing
tearing scars all up the trunk where fronds
break off, year after year. A large green lizard,
a chameleon, lurks and snaps his tongue
at insects, doves devour seeds and rockets
soar overhead. It all feels natural
and some may be — the bird before she was
a symbol, the changing reptile, me
here, the enemy firing ceaselessly.

LOVE POEMS

For Susann, Twenty-eight Years

More than I am anything else —
sailor, pirate, flesh-eating koala,
Jew, poet, gardener, philosopher,
chef, father, or all the other
sweetnesses that have gathered, I am that man
standing, sitting, lying next to Susann.

I do not always stand erect or sit up straight.
In first grade, in the Bronx, I got "unsatisfactory"
in Posture, on an otherwise fine report card,
and I have slouched since, like a half-trained vine.

Susann dances and sings, so even her slouch
has such grace that I, lurching beside her seem
almost tall, a bit lithe, sometimes, foolishly,
I try to skip, or smile and croak out a tune.

For Susann

Nature is what dies, not all at once
but all the parts we live in, and us.
So I shall not be a poet of nature
embellishing memories of manured
roses and lilies. I have never been
"half in love" with death or ever thought
of it as "easeful." The always changing
seas and hills have nothing to do with me.
Like the city, they are just there for now.
Like us. I sit in our house. Barely,
just green tuft in the bottom of my window,
the neighbors' young lime tree, shows beneath
the aluminum frame. Bookcases, sixty shelves
around me and downstairs are filled with time,
like hills and seas we've made. They will last
longer than the lime tree. A sunbird.
iridescent blue, hovers above a lime flower.
I know he is beautiful and hungry and think
to call Susann. We can watch it start to die,
to die this day's death which I hope is not
his last. I do not call her. I am not
a nature poet. When I could, I planted gardens
and tended them. Thirty-three years ago,
crossing an urban field, a vacant lot, really,
with Susann, I stopped and saw flowering weeds
not ankle high, tiny yellow blossoms
and even smaller white ones, and clover, too.
The green weeds shone, that had been raggedy

the week before, before Susann. All that day
I was not dying, and there have been other
immortalities. Yes, I have been a nature poet
from time to time, when nature stands still.

For Susann, Thirty-one Years

We are grown-ups now
not adults, never that;
we play in grown-up clothes
and play gets real, but skin
stays soft, your great brown eyes
like ox-eyed Hera's and our ancient minds
uncluttered, I sit in books of poems,
thousands, and some are mine
and you. Our nursery rhymes
grow nuanced but the pure
rhythms and words remain.

Our grandson, Ashrei, squalls
downstairs. He may become
adult. I hope not, for his sake
and for his sister's and for aging us,
not adult — only grow-up.

PERICHORESIS: FOR SUSANN ON OUR THIRTY-THIRD ANNIVERSARY

Dionysian revels are so far behind us
we need no Tristram's blade to lie between
in space where we lie parallel, but through your flesh
I think or feel I see a trace of light,
or it may be a hope or afterglow
of image I remember from a book.
I say it's real, that we have passed into
what's after love, that doesn't have a name,
and I am Yeats's bird, perhaps a pigeon,
a golden ruse upon a thin old limb
that chirps and tweets and croaks and, listen, coos
"Of what is past and passing and to come."

A Valentine

My young wife is growing old she says
undone by humility and shame, hurting
as women do, the beautiful ones,
mirror flattered, unadorned.

My wife is twenty-two, feet in a field
of flowering weeds, crossing a lot,
or kneeling by the English daisies.
Her eyes are larger than eyes.

My young wife soothes my old skin
with uncalloused hands. Her mind is clouded
with infirmity. She does not know that she
is young forever, even in winter.

AUBADE

This should be light, for you were
leaning against me, your hands
breezes, your heavier hands and lips
gusted me to sleep, deep sleep,
after a nightmare year
so there was calm in you, a still
that is already gone.

I am not light,
Lady, as this should be. I
have been storm too long, breaking
dark after dark, screaming
unmetaphorically.

This
should be light, but barely,
like the dawn you left in,
marked by the morning's memory
of just faded stars,
like a new wind deciding
around, you, lovely,
whether to rise or fall.

FOR EVA

My sister-in-law's gone mad.
Telephones crackle beams at her with sniper's skill
a stranger's sneeze bursts on her ears
from blocks away. She hears doors slam
in other houses. Chirp by chirp the early angel birds
tear at her head.
But not mine, except the crows.
Eva at twenty-one, a pianist
on tour in Europe, drugged and sexy,
in a letter, advised my wife — all she had to say —
"Do not fake orgasm." Do not make those sounds
unless you mean them, groan by moan.

Eva sleeps in airports or at train
stations, cacophony hiding noise.
Dropped coins don't ring in the clamor
single notes and chords do not confound.

Sanity is singular, living with singularity
and separations. The mad are single hopelessly,
separated from others' separateness.

Crows caw at all hours. Each cry pierces.
In winter, the nests fill tree crotches,
withstand every wind, support all snow.

Eva's gone mad. The sound of a stranger passing
scratching his head undoes her. The faucet —

even silent — is a threat. And roots stretching in soil,
ice hardening, email tumbling in space,
the black thought of the communal crows.

For Kathy

An artist in California. She died many years ago, apparently of
anorexia nervosa.

I knew you were essential when we kissed
intense, brief, and with a muse's chasteness
but not a child's. To hold you was to hold
not space but time, not after the manner
of women. Afterward all memory was gone.

Not Aphrodite's beauty but a way
of looking made men mad. We traded poems
for paintings over fruit and wine. Husband
nor wife could comprehend that consummation.
We made love without touching. We were angels.

My brother-in-law called and said the place
of your body was gone. He does not know
(and often I forget) how time is held
in color, words and form, that memory
but never what is real can ever die.

For my Father

Beer Sheva 5739

What a joke this would have been
on Father! He brought me up
to be a gentleman — I still can't eat
naturally, and scold my children
when they do. I can still read Catullus
Ovid, Horace (applied to schools
like an Episcopalian, though attended
NYU). Learned Hebrew, too,
more Mother that. And here I am
in boor land, screaming at clerks
and pushing onto buses, praying
like a greenhorn on Grand Street,
bargaining over every pair of shoes,
pondering *midrashim* and *mishnayes*
that got old crazy Uncle Abe
fired six times in seven years
from banks, butcher shops, and even
Hebrew publishers in the Jewish Bronx.

Father, we eat well at home,
the books are bound in boards,
the children are obedient as you wished,
even to different laws.
The local wines are potable,
except when drunk I'm ceremonious —
and the ceremonies are old, Dad, old.

For Our Thirty-seventh Wedding Anniversary

Frog's sodden planks have rooted in this soil,
the wood returned to trees that grew upright
in the southern planted forests forty years
ago, chopped down and dried and planed
and fashioned into craft, the *Frog* we sailed
down *wadi* into freedom, piratical
but laughing. Shall these boards live? We chortle now
the tears have dried, but not the opened eyes.
Love is as good to move as wind or any tide
a vessel of the mind. After the storms
of setting out, the facing gales, we sail
almost at peace, watchful but not wary
hearing the palm doves coo, the bulbuls' songs
from where *Frog's* spars are branches, where they throng.

For Susann at Fifty-seven

I never was all youthful dewy-eyed
excitement, fledgling, tuneful, arms
impatient, wrapping inexpert new
around a figure thought of (was it me?)
as you were when we met. I did not think
to live so very long, to wish you happy
older than I was then, thirty-four years
ago, most of your life so far, your brown
eyed beauty still or more so, now dark greens
and barely pebbled skin against my gray
and rock rough brain, no more spring lightness
and yielding soft as padded silk in May
I never merited, already full of what
I was then, and am now, waiting for you.

FOR SUSANN ON HER SIXTY-FOURTH BIRTHDAY

May 29, 1953.

Hillary and Tenzing
stared out at the lower world from above
standing on Mt. Everest, four years before
the birth of Susann, and in her natal year
Elvis Presley writhed on US TV,
Laura Ingalls Wilder went to a little grave
in Missouri and Bergman's "Seventh Seal"
debuted in Stockholm, with Susann way down south
in Gothenburg, born to the sad survivors
of Nazi terror. In the US,
Allen Ginsberg's "Howl" was called obscene
and it is, but holy too, and I've taught it
as both. John Lennon met Paul McCartney
and "On the Road" made minds change.
Susann lived in her sad and quiet world
a younger sister, in a seaport refuge, while
"West Side Story" lit up Broadway. Sputnik
circled the Earth. Then Laika was the first
skeleton in space. I was seventeen. I studied
hard and learned a little, lived in America
in its gold years. I awaited Susann then
in those lonely, sad, and wasted decades.

The deep pink roses bloom now over the red
and white snapdragons. Susann is sixty-four
and I blow out my candles, eighty-one,
while we still laugh and touch and mock
our overcome impossibilities, gaze
from a private peak, higher than Himalayas.

I Awake

Lips flutter by my ear. The morning's cool
and I wake to Susann's breath, a minty warmth,
and laugh ahead to her, back at the boring
horror of dreams she vanishes, broken years
she folds and puts away. I wake to eyes
too large for simple sight. An endless brown
all earth grown knowing opens over me.
Her wingtip fingers touch me into song
and into thoughts of empty time to come
which Susann names unsmiling while we kiss.
She leaves to tremble forward into day,
I stay to wrap these words around us with
my stolid lips and eyes, my creaking hands
spread poems on the neatly folded years.

IF YOU...

If only you would simper or be younger
yet, or if the little leopard in your eyes
who plays at hunting wouldn't, or if your head
didn't lean forward towards me when we talk
I might be grown avuncular and say,
"It all will be alright, dear," pat your hand
and be polite and caring just enough.
I wouldn't want to take you in both arms
and tease the fearful beast to leap on me
and tear my world to pure erotic bits
we'd sit and nibble. Woman, child, you
are danger beautifully wrapped and make
me think when I was. Stretching, some old cat
awakes in me, and it will be alright.

On the Anniversary of my Father's Death, I Sit in the Spring Garden

Flowers color every nook and crevice
pots of ranunculus and freesia erupt
asking to be cut to bless our tables
and birds I have not met sing loudly
tunes butterflies dance to.
A faint scent as if from far away.
My Father would have loved this in his life
and I offer it here to his spirit.

Part of an Elegy for Henry Codish (1960-1965)

1

Your death made stronger love
(not that your life diminished it)
but all death does that.
For all that you will never forgive
we magnified and forgave each other;
in the suspension of your breath
was the necessity that ours be shared.
I do not cite this as purpose or need
for the terror of your blue example.

2

The moon and the sea have a working agreement
for reciprocal interaction: no love there.
It is the grass, which takes everything from the sun —
lives in its light because of its light, greens in it,
grows, browns, does nothing for its love but give reason,
one of many, that, feeling itself loved, must love:
not the reaching tide and purposeful moon, which give,
grown, but the grass, sun's child; giftless, helpless, taking.

3

What we found was a cold blue body
face down in a pillow. Cyndi's cry:
"Henry's dead!" Then knowledge shut out,
pleadings to get up, slaps, threats,

oxygen; the doctor called asking
over and over not, "Is he dead?"
but "Is he alive?"
    And I, spreading
the snot-clogged, teeth-clenched mouth
to work, with my lungs, a chest
that would never work itself;
crying into the tearless eyes:
not for them, but for futility.

4

Let no one personify death
for sleep is no brother to it,
lovemaking no little sister.
It is like nothing else, but not
like nothing: the gray rocks
are not dead, nor the long
sewn corpses. The undertaker,
the days, the brown hole in the grass:
what do these have to do with then —
the time when knowledge and object
are one word, and that word is dead.

5

I must write this for you now,
and mourn, and set it aside;
for there are other children, sons
and daughters, and they will live
in our house and in our love.
They will see your picture and be
bemused. They will force us,
with a question, to hurry

through your existence, not wanting them
to know that children die.

6

If there is love and purpose;
not in the world, not in intrigues
and strangers, whose lives and deaths
are rumors, or a friend's
story at night, but here, then;
in this house, in this grasp
of taste and color and words
are five years meaning.

Joy has no more of feeling
than iridescence has color
and is as brief
as the time between desires;
is the waterfall a rainbow makes
but not the sky;
your kissing your mother
on cheeks and eyes.

Understanding, we love and hate
by turns, and our chosen word
is a balance, a tree with many
branches, some of which are dead.
A child's love is a promise
to grow, which you kept always,
to show that hate and tears,
weakness and misunderstanding,
knowledge, and even death,
are not love's opposites,
but only other things.

Sheila at Fifty-seven

Would she have wrinkled more
than this imagining, put weight
on the slim frame she died in?
I dust black hair I cut
shorter, older. Her grass green silk
gold lace at cuffs and collar
in thirty years has faded
to hay and rust.

At fifty-five
I could not see her clear
she was so skin soft
lithe and walked by then
too fast for me, was shy perhaps
of brother bald and fat,
stumbling beside her.

I have to age her so
we can embrace.

My sister's flesh is loose now
like my own, she rises slowly
listens with more care and sees
through thicker glass.

We talk and laugh.
Our youthful voices merge.

This year you cough more.
Your face concludes a weariness
where memory ends. I hold you up
but not forever. Only
our voices will never change.

Poem at Sixty-one

The moon is a hard ball of rock
held in orbit by gravity
and reflects light

The yellow marigolds
bend downward massed
artificially

In the next room my children
the first dilution of my
immortality of my germ cells

Once I knew more colors
than I knew names
now azure and cerulean are blue

Susann soothes skin I touch
with my fingertips
roughness smoothly

My mind stumbles
when it runs
tripping through thought.

The Lime Tree Flowers on Karen's Birthday

In Nisan, citrus scents our gardens
even in plague time, intoxicating,
and I think of you and our first meeting
in my plague time, and your being
was like the odor of the lime tree
separating horror and beauty.

For Lenny Galliulo

Who said he wouldn't live past 35

1967.
Dirt curtained room
grass, booze and lesson plans
installation art
drum sets and wire spool tables
two Mafioso friends of yours
in rumpled suits and serious ties
complaining about long hours
over rabbit and pasta
the cheapest red wine
in New York State
Karen adoring me
Fran cooking
our students in the background
worshipping you
who taught them what they never knew
they had to know.

At the Lion you
ten minute drums alone
Tom on bass
four years before he hanged himself
the robed stripper
drinking with me
talking about her kids
no glass clinked
you were that good.

From a Letter to Lenny

He decides to live to be 40

Like you friend, I live with guilt as with
a beautiful woman. Who sees always?
Sometimes bravura motion, her sweet flow
from corridor to room, her reshaped turns
of hip or throat, bending to make the bed,
inserting slivered garlic in the roast,
won't matter like results, neatness and taste.
A woman lovely young is lovely old
and lovely middle-aged; and also guilt
stays sharp but skin gets hard. The puckered scar
with soft sore center answers poke or kiss
with pulse more even back then when she was
the first or tenth time entered, closes down
or spreads, Lenny, redder and wittily.

Bad Sleep

Survivors dream; they shouldn't,
dreams are lies. I'll never be
anyone's child again. Angel go away,
the light s out, I killed it,
time is now. I'm strong enough
to wrestle with myself. Why drag me back?
I'll rip your wings, I'll punch your name out, break —
I can't wake up, that knee
crunches between my legs. Let go!
I'll tell you, but it isn't true
this dream, I'm all grown up. I am.

Never to wash the crease
behind my ears again, or scrub
that washrag's toughness
in my throat, school's over
for me, the last green vegetable,
the final piece of liver
eaten, and my teeth unbrushed.
Free to curse my sister,
to put my shoes on the bed,
stay up all night, pick flowers
from the neighbors' lawns. My toys
are all over the floor, I didn't
take my medicine. Later,
in the park, I'll pound
Robby to a pulpy mess,
step, on my way home,

on every crack, take
a comic book from the drugstore,
if the owner catches me.
Mom's dead, I'll cry,
who can you call?

For Rosalyn

I am not my sister or anything like,
I used to reassure myself,
money was not my goal I said and said
in my wooden hut, eating noodles
and state subsidized cottage cheese,
beating a rat to death under the tiny
refrigerator, while our daughter
smiled in her nearby crib.

When lack of money drove us out of Zion
back to America, you took us in, four
of us by then, and we huddled
proud and lying, around a table
built of memory. Alan was good
but too victorious for me, the house
gloriously American, the children
suburban superstars.

For twenty years we worked
and invested money, and thrived
as Americans do, if they
are white, smart, educated
and keep track, unlike their dogs
of how many bones we have.

So you were right, and Alan was, but not
completely. Our parents raised us both;
I thank you now for what
you learned from them, and flick
this poem across the years. Eat, if you want.

Love, Ed

JEMIMAH

And he called the name of the first Jemimah....
Job 42.14

Squalling in her crib, her diaper soaked,
her red face twisted between clenched fists
and her wrinkled legs drawn to her belly like a frog's,
she waves her mouth around, looking for a tit
as if the world were hunger.

MY CHILDREN

Seven have vanished
in death, divorce, hatred,
and I have a daughter
Idit Miriam, who is still
an infant. She is a smile
now, she can't think.

IDIT

sleeps in her red carriage,
in beads and rattles
dressed all in pink and green
like the garden, with seed heads.

A Muse
in wet diapers, at best,
an incoherent oracle
predicting change.

Leaving Room

Almost all the black
lily-deep earth
under viburnum
or where viburnum was before the white
creeping trunk eaters
laced inch-thick wood that crumpled
to my daughter's tug
and left sprigs in the air only
of white-lace flowers
is covered now, June,
with salvia, small begonias,
mints and impatiens.

Seedlings swarm in flowerpots
on the porch steps, or crowd the bed
under the kitchen window.
There is room beneath the viburnum
or around the shoots of viburnum,
bending weak wood.

I keep one bookcase empty.
I do not teach my daughter
everything I know.

Sleep Song

An arrow thunked and shook itself to sleep
above the waterline; two others hissed
over our huddled heads into white foam:
I paddled out of bowshot into calm
while you looked up adoring, your long hair
spread all around my feet, your face pressed close
about my knees, your arm stretched out to reach
the muscles in my back, above my waist.

I think you were my sister. I was eight
years old or less. You may have been a picture
in a book, you had no name or history.
Every night I thought of different ways
to come to land, remove your soggy clothes,
wash your bruises, cuddle by the flame
under the blanket spread on mattressed leaves
in purity I made myself believe.

A curve of arm or eyebrow shakes my sleep.
I nock an arrow to the sinew strung
on tightened oak. The children splutter by
as usual, their leaky boat kept floating
by their fright and innocence. I twang out
a song and threat to speed them on their way,
roll over, close my eyes, I touch my wife,
and chase my aging want of lust downdream.

So Far Today...

Is this a poem I ask iambically
more or less as here so far today
my wife Susann has brought to bed for me
three cups of coffee and two slices, thick,
of chocolate cake she baked and then weeded
the garden I planned she planted while I turned
pages of books she carried from the post
and called my friend who's editing my poems
for one big book of me. The Syrian
hibiscus blasts out blue and yellow
flowering shrubs say here's September
and caterpillars look for twigs to spin
out their cocoons. Is this a worthy song
to end a book with, or just a love list
of my fortune, lying old and crippled
cared for and edited, almost happy.

NEW YEAR 5782

I am as old as the Jewish century
Ed Codish (570 – who knows?)
but probably not many more. It's judgment day
as if every day was not, were not.
I made a pact with Susann that I'd never
die and leave her gardening alone
setting the table for herself and wandering
the empty upstairs hallway and my study
full of books that interested only me.
Instead I have to live another year
and then another, like Robert Frost
with his snowy horse and promises to keep.

Washing Clothes at Bar-Ilan University

I drank too much last night this morning
my head hurts and I roam around
Susann is doing the laundry
the red russelia warms the air
wilts and dries in the heat it hangs in
jasmine whitens the scented day
the sky acacia and rosewood bleed to
Susann sorts through purple blouses
bright blue dresses and dark blue socks
large and brown and mild her eyes are
disapproving but still we kiss
black barred white winged crimson hoopoes
peck in the grass and soar away
the first flamboyant trees drip scarlet
flowers over my humid face
water lilies afloat in the pond
wash my eyes while Susann washes
colors we muddied yesterday
hot and smiling Susann finishes
comes to me in the cleanest sun

INTENSITIES

HAIKU

One ash escapes my rake
and the fire of spring leaf burning.
First butterfly!

A Very Short Poem About How I Feel Today at Three in the Afternoon

A white dragon tears at my thigh
sharp fangs at first then slowly gnawing teeth
like molars grinding. A mix of drugs
and mindless writing helps.
Lava hot dragon slime hurts.

INTENSITIES

For Michael, Shlomo, David, Aliza, Batsheva and Asaf
You could have sailed with me, there always is
clearance, and permission to come aboard.
Now *Frog's* in a far harbor, anchor down,
tuned to a frequency you do not know,
crewed by strong sailors, captain and a mate
who've dared and lost or won. For now I bless:
Love and goodbye.

A NEW DOG

A brown and white mongrel
nine months old
a large mutt colored
desert camouflage. He should live
fourteen years. He is
my last dog, I at eighty.
I am pale white,
perhaps, I fear,
hospital camouflage.
He licks my hand
I stroke his head.
He cannot count and I
would rather not.

GETTING STABLE

Drained as unfolded seabed
ancient, where stone bones
of fossil fish
slowly swim through rock
whose strata float on time,
cold as the ice that covers
that moving mountain,
empty and unharmed
as the space outside
atoms the sun spits, filthy
to the darkness, stark,
between the stars.

How Morning Glories Cover a Fence

In late spring, your mother dies. Soon after, your marriage ends and you move to a small wooden house with a wire fence outside the front door. On the outside of the fence, in sandy, loamy soil, you plant morning glory seeds you have soaked in water overnight. You plant them in groups of three, about eight inches apart. After a week or so, they sprout. When they sprout, invite your children to see them. Describe what will happen as they grow. Talk to them about your Mother, that she loved flowers. Do not talk about your wife. When they return to their mother, thin the sprouts so only one out of the three, the largest and strongest, is left. You may, in front of the morning glories, plant portulacas to bejewel the sandy ground. The morning glories will now reach the lowest links of the wire fence. With thin twine, attach the stems of the vines to the wires. The morning glory vines will begin to twine about the structure of the fence. They will branch out and wind about each other. Show this to the children when next they visit. Let them touch, gently, the rapid growth. After three months, the morning glories will begin to flower, to make the fence a cool, deep blue from dawn to midday. Make sure the children see this, and the portulaca meadow.

I Look at a Garden I Am Too Feeble to Walk About In

The long red stem covered with small pink flowers
and the hundred others swaying in a breeze
my face feels, and I too sway, slow as my age
and weight and heavy lonely thoughts.

Sonnet: Suppose There Were One Spring

Suppose there were one spring, no other chance
for April, in years as it is in men;
no turning, recurring warmth to wait for.
Who would stay all summer? Cowards? Optimists?
One took all my warmth, and gave it away,
when I was great and strode in cities.
I rage in autumn at my distant sun.
This is epiphenominal, like the world's
second death. There is not even tragedy
to make men gasp, and think and stumble home.
Some years ago I lacked the courage for that.
I am Antigone, married to another,
or Antony, embracing Caesar's knees
and made governor of a barren Western land.

Squeeze

Jerry and Rita, reciprocally,
I hope and, carefully from the bottom,
toothpaste and unguents, so far it's good
but pythons squeeze, and wrestlers and the bank
if one owes it money. I wonder if the sound
is what the victims make, not Rita
or Jerome, who sort of hum in pleasure.
The mob and lovers have in common
closeness, the press of flesh that means.

This Is the Fourth Generation

Bloodied, in three years, twelve seasons.
My father, his father
and a cousin preceded you.
You make a small, strange, masculine
company in my brain.

Buried in my Garden

So many dead are buried here
in the small flower covered space
between the house and the hewn stone wall.
My Father's sister and his brother
and their young sons,
my Mother's sisters and her brother,
and Father and Mother,
my sister, all alone
in my longing and grief,
a five year son, and most
of my classmates, some students too, young, young,
and two beloved friends
out of the few who've loved me.
A white rose rambles over bones.
The foxgloves and hibiscus feed
on blood and sinew, muscles that moved earth
and heaven too, when my mind touched their souls.
Barking dead dogs and cats insinuating
lie here too, between the wooden door
and the first stones, spirits of love, immortal
because they never thought of death.
An olive tree is full of birds that soar
heavenward, singing this news.

Children's Story

Her name was Janice; often after school
we'd sit and talk, cosmogonize,
with skill and art a minor
god might envy,
hold hands, touch arms and shoulders,
sometimes kiss, more often
arrange a habitation in the world
we made, remade, and as the winter passed
made and remade again. How we could know,
sixteen years old, American
and comfortable that
the world we lived in never would be worth
repair or rehabilitation I
don't understand or ever will. Sweet nihilists,
we stroked and chatted all that world away.
In February, snow fell clotted thick
and settled in her hair. The white and red
she shook out running spun us home to bed
unwitting but most simple and most good
we trembled and we laughed
we were transfigured, moments,
into the best of all
the garden fictions we were masters of.

CHILDREN'S STORY, 2

My father came home late that day, the snow
had sat down wet and slushed, the three of us
talked hours, ate, my father quickly drank,
looking at us and hearing angels breathe
deeply after angels thoughtless doing,
most of a quart of scotch. At ten or so
her parents called her home; my father took
his car keys out, he juggled them, he wouldn't
hear of taxicabs or long dark, walks; we went
sometimes on all four wheels, or two or three
sliding from curb to curb.
He showed us fear for showing him a world
he'd had to swerve away from.
Or did we force a prophecy to rise
in him against the liquor's power?
It is a wonder that we weren't killed
and a pity.

CRASH

I'm all raged out. The pieces lie around
for miles — unbodied arms and thighs, the ash
of children's toys, whole heads and parts of house
ruined on the ground, destroyed by fire and
the great explosion, where I fell. "Experts
combed the wreckage," I read, "for the black box,"
the bloodless voice that stutters final words,
as if words helped, ever, after the end.

DRAGON POEM

Gold and green and a roaring dragon
before the black
and the mourners' clattering comfort.
Water wells, but angry tears hold back
in hatred of the thirsty earth.
Cousins try the questions of death —
Did he suffer? Did you know
it would come?

I cannot weep.
I heard the dragon roar
so green and cold
as if it were April,
I cannot speak
for there is no connecting
here of sound and care.

If you loved, look:
trees cluster leaves no more
but, leaf, leaf, leaf;
each different, and each
a different green, strange
on the same separated twig
for you to make a pattern of,
for the dragon to burn.

For Wislawa Szymborska

"The body is a reservoir of pain"

"The Nightmarish Contingency of Human Survival"
whatever that means.

Clouds half shield heaven
though leafless trees point up
and only some thoughts bounce
back off the stratocumulus.

I read it, cited from *The New Yorker,*
on the back cover of New Poems and Collected
by Wislawa Szymborska and then
studied the poems, most of them.

I have to teach in a few minutes,
Kundera's *The Unbearable Lightness of Being,*
to a class of seventeen year olds,
most of them lovely
whose minds penetrate the texts
glancing, ricocheting off words
and chapters. Much breaks through
distorted by contingency
perhaps, but certainly surviving.
"The body is a reservoir of pain"
well dammed. Mostly it holds.

BEGINNINGS

Before he learned
to tell time
time told
him.

This is not like mourning for a father.
Remembering a child is all color and motion,
half taught but wholly learned.

Friday Afternoon, I Open the Front Door, I Feel Very Old

Pain in my back spreads wide
across from hip to hip
I stand at the open front door
watching the breeze stir the Stippa grass
and rattle the blood red Gaura spears
stabbing the sweet scented air.
My wife is beautiful in the kitchen
marinating artichoke hearts
the almond tree is shade and nesting room
and later food for men and birds.
If I can get upstairs, forcing a smile
I'll nap before guests and dinner.

Again Consider the Embarrassment of Old Age

Now while I think of the flowering garden,
the white rose flowers on the wall vine
Armeyria surrounding white callas
voices rising laughing up the stairs
I lie on my back deep in my imagination.
The boat I built in mind is full of friends
floating through spring fields
on surges of deep water.

Poem at Sixty-five

In Miss Nichol's fifth grade class
the class where I learned everything —
Greeks and Romans, the Middle Ages,
and Europe, how we won, and studied maps in red
(England)
and green, I think (French)
and blue (us). The Greeks were virtue, Persia oriental
slavery. She loved Athens, Pericles and Plato.
When Sparta crumbled the long walls,
we felt the draft in the classroom.

I began to add the years. In 2000, I would be sixty.
It seemed unlikely.

In the Hundred Years War, we rooted for England.
In religious wars, in Germany,
even the Italian and Polish kids wanted
Gustavus Adolphus to win. We evolved
on a great colored chart with us
on the top, blond, long-haired, fur-clad.

The Germans were Persian. The Russians
were farther down the chart,
with the Indians and Goths.
At recess, I mapped my classmates, the boys.
I wasn't sure where the girls went.

We pledged allegiance; we declaimed

The Lord's Prayer; we stood in line.
Each desk declared my praise, each seat
ranked and filed from the front to the back and right to left
from me, the best (next to the door front right)
to the grisly shame of the untrainable
in the far left back. Except for Alfred
the right side of the room was Jewish
as a ghetto after nightfall.
Barbarians laughed behind us,
far away from us.

I am almost sixty-five. It is hard to bend.
Weeds encroach on my garden;
insects ravage the cherry blossoms.

My eyes are bifocaled; my teeth are plastic;
I am fat and slow; other parts do not
yield former pleasures.

I have five thousand books. Miss Nichols
taught me to read them, to connect
book to book in multiples and to connect
multiples to multiples. Ideas
form and tangle, untangle.
They nourish me.

I am almost sixty-five. It is still
unlikely. My desk wobbles
a bit, the wood is warped,
the ink well almost dry. The school is long
torn down; we have all evolved.
I cling, fierce, to my place
in front, on the right side.

The Battered Cat

For Tom B.

When we sat in the park
the whores brought you strawberries
and would have brought themselves

Your double bass made dark
music white man drunk
each night in the cheap
salesmen club and then

nights at home you beat the cat
hurled the beast
downstairs and followed
screaming kicking
and the cat bled
from mouth ears eyes rectum
yowled and yowled
and you blinded it
finally
swung hard sobbing on a wall
so the cat died the night
your housemate Lenny
my drummer friend
threw you out
the night you took a knife
and cut his drums

And I paid for my son's
recorder lessons
with soup and sandwiches
and the whores loved you too
and the devil never played
better double bass
Tom you never had twenty dollars
all together in your life

and the cat loved you never
left and Tom you could play bass

A letter after years
from Lenny
says you hanged yourself
somewheres in Arkansas
Tom your blind old cat
always forgave you.
That death was an accident.

Intensive Care

There were the big numbers of blood pressure
and, on the right, the small numbers
of blood pressure, and the oscilloscope
whose top curve was heart beat rate
that read out on its own display above
and all this was repeated on other dials
where the nurses sat at the bright green
patient control center watching and
listening to the hisses beeps buzzers
and the gong that meant run!
Some machine or tube or patient
has malfunctioned or stopped.

My mother raised three children, worked
as a bookkeeper, kept
everything adjusted and running well
but never had to operate a system
as complicated as this one. With
no practice at all, or even lessons,
she ran it for a week and a half,
made all the wavy white lines move
just so, the numbers float and flash
the way the doctor said. She
never talked or even looked at me
she was so busy and responsible,
and buzzed, hissed, cried and finally died.

THE LIMITS OF MEDICINE

An instant every morning, long
or small, always an instant
between waking and remembering,
I am happy. Why? Do dreams
so cure, is everyone still alive
in dreams? My father, my sister,
my mother, my son? Am I
sober in my dreams? Sane?
Do I not rave and rage, torture
my wife and children, friends,
and other people still alive
in my dreams? Then why's the pillow
wet, the blanket twisted
like rope, why do I cry No!
in my sleep? Do I fight hard
not to wake up? With whom?
What angel comes to put love in
and why can't I hold him there
with muscles or with tears? He goes
and leaves me with a moment's peace,
The day wears it away, instantly.
I can take pills or drink to keep
from hurting, but can find nothing,
though I look long and deep, to keep
from knowing that hurt.

There Is a White Butterfly

Despair was listening to baseball on the radio,
picking the phone up and not using it,
sleeping till noon on workdays, throwing
the mail away unread. I miss all that.

Now, despair is drinking myself to sleep
or hate, at day's end, waking at 3 AM
and no late movie, soon, nothing to eat.
The mailman hasn't been around in weeks.

There is a white butterfly on the marigold
and no one to show it to. Maybe brain cancer
would get me out of this, or you will,
or some other masturbatory fantasy.

I look at the white butterfly on the marigold
its black mouth buried in that tangerine;
the blue veined wings, unsynchronized, are wavering,
the compound eyes see everything, except ahead.

Emotional Direction

To go from rage into despair is sideways
somewhere near the bottom, and sexual desire
is in the middle, with hallways in and out
to most other locations, except
depression, most of which is on the floor
and the rest in my office. Love squats at home
or staggers who knows where. Joy's out of town
this month, I got a letter, living with someone else.
Fear pays the rent and visits late at night
upstairs with hate, I hear them move together,
and I am jealous even of that mismatch
here in the living room, watching loneliness
grope at my intellect like a fourteen year old boy
whose daddy bought him a whore for his birthday.

Pharmacy

I have ingested eleven pills so far
this morning, and it is early. Soon,
another and then no more 'til after-
noon. Blood pressure, cholesterol, and
above all pain, three kinds of pills, together,
let me limp along and smile and pet the dog
and stay alive. Who might have lived of those
who like my Father died for lack of pills
or Mother, sister, son? What charge to merit
that I still write their lives and mine and more,
my blood infused with years of science since
they stopped their nurturing, and made me owe
line after line, the sentencing to sentence
after sentence, smiles, steps, a life, a happiness.

Camden 1950s

A song of myself,
Jeffrey and Louis and Shirley and
Sheila and Rosalyn and Sheila
Asher and Debby and Lynn,
Robert and Nathan and others whose
names I forget and the dogs
Rusty and Ruffles and Buster
who had a small hole in the top of his skull
and Chips and some more who came from another block
to Belleview Avenue,
a mile and a half from Walt Whitman's house
and two blocks from school.

Beth El was at one end
Orthodox Sons of Israel
around the corner.

Half way towards Beth El
two witches painted stone steps weekly
white or red or white-veined
fieldstone gray. They cackled as they drew
their brushes back and forth.

The tiny yards were weeds
or fads of rocks and marigolds. The street at evening
was stickball and curses in Yiddish
or later, kisses and rumors of more.
On rickety porches of little houses

parents sat. We all had time
then in that village.

Tattooed women at *shul*
stuffed cakes in pockets
cold cuts up their sleeves. The principal
spoke with a German accent we thought
Yiddish so we laughed
at him, we laughed him away.

When colored people started to move in
we learned that when a dog shits
on a colored neighbor's lawn
it's on purpose.

Walt Whitman's house was still
a mile and a half away but school was
close. He was the myth of movies
to school's TV, real and educational.
On our school's pilgrimage

Miss Osborne read "O Captain
My Captain" in a feeling thrill
and I didn't listen. The park
across the street was full of queers.

Miss Nichol's blue-white hair unruffled,
her anger made us silenter than stones.
We did line up. We quivered.
She taught me everything —
to learn and love to. She would be fired now
for calling Annie stupid and for mocking
Robert's weeks of work on ancient Greece

as "crude and sloppy." My sisters sobbed
and went to other teachers. Not me.

Silhouettes of being marched
undisciplined through mind.

Ten years old
walking barefoot and in shorts
past Gloria's house and Gloria
and Renee laughing, pointing
so I ran in my head away but walked and spat
at Renee's withered arm, that polio summer.
(Gloria in a car years later
reaching for me, but I still hated her.)

Alfred pitied me for being smart
and not athletic, I sat by the door
he in the far back corner. Miss Brown arranged us
weekly by our rank and chair by measured chair
and child by quiet child
(it seemed God's seating chart)
we knew who we were.
I loved my clear first place.
My father's mother slouched
in her slip on the porch. I reddened for her.

Suicide Note

I think I'll join my dead, that doesn't mean
the world's not funny.

      Loveliness still moves
around me now, lantana blossoms yellow
and roots deep, full breasted girls go belly
flop and sputter out of water, shaking
my eyes and resolution. A sparkling wine
condenses vapor on my glass's bowl
and buzzes in my head. Leg muscles stretch,
my drying arms are tight, I will go down
in comfort, feeling good. The pills I need
lie in the shade beside me, players hit
balls back and forth and laugh, my children watch
and chase each other shrieking but they're not
enough.

      They all wait for me, I'm going.

Nihil ex Nihilo Fit

The green Duranta leaves and deep blue flowers
and Susann dressed in green, her face a flower
tinged in the palest blue whenever she walks
the garden there, and polished ivory
where the six-foot tall Abelia half in sun
half shadows her. When Susann sings the bright
blue sunbird sings, I hear him, and so sex
makes sacred song of Sabbath burst a world
of garden to our table. Nothing from
empty vastness, but the smallest speck
can fill a world, this butterfly creates
the color white and movement, food and drink
connecting blue Duranta, white Abelia
and me and Susann and by this poem.
You too. Let's call beginnings God. Why not?

HUMORESQUE

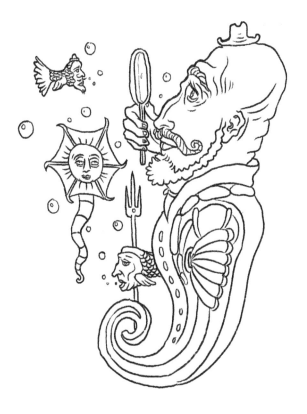

AFTER SEPTEMBER 11,
OR: PLEASE MUZZLE YOUR FLAGS

I am bitten by flags
moored in earth and cars
and on lapels, pasted on windows,
flying from bicycles,
choked by AIDS ribbons,
gay ribbons,
breast cancer ribbons,
by Armenian Massacre ribbons —
gored by Jew buttons and Goy buttons —
maybe poet buttons
if all the colors weren't taken.
(Are there any Terrorist ribbons
black for nihilism, red for revolt?)
Does the empty breasted flagless man or woman
favor terror and disease?
I wear a blank button. I wave
a flag without design
and without teeth.

Again for my Students

Whenever one of my students goes mad
I feel annoyed, the sense I get when a dog
I've trained refuses to fetch and runs dog fast
away with the ball or stick. Sometimes
one finds out new directions and never
does come back. Somewhere slobber seeps
down a lesson. Oh return already
the real skill is in the throwing. Anyone
can follow the high hurl, the spinning toss.
I could have taught you that. You're not a dog.

Up Yours

Ah, dear
no, I'll
never ac-
cept the
way we
left. Love
and fate
should not
so differ that filling
out of either leaves the other
so bereft. To snaggle-molared destiny that sought
to chew the heart I offered from my love and
spew the shining pieces on the
further side of my soul, I say,
Do not go soon away, but linger.
Though you may not have my
heart, see, I offer you my finger.

Deer Throw Ecosystem into Chaos

"Varmints of old were mainly predators, " Dr. McShea
said, *"but this is the age of the marauding herbivore."*
New York Times, December 11, 2002

You are a marauding herbivore,
nibbling away my hemlocks,
stunting my cedars
into bonsai. Your molars grind hungry
in my hair, strip all my bark.

I try what everyone tries
sharpshooting, trapping, birth-control
darts, repellents, and other tactics
to the usual avail. I also write
to your mother, ask the cops
for restraining orders, plant crops known
to repel your kind. I put bad music
on the stereo, don't wash, leer inanely
at the ninety-three year old man
next door.

It is "a browser's paradise"
in my well-watered world. The tender branchlets
on this tree of life are nudely rudely gnawed.

I might grow antlers
in simple self-defense.

"Deer are drawing cougars ever eastward,"
comforts the *New York Times*
and one of us is going to get eaten
first.

Busyness

I have never been busy. No day has ever passed without time for
me to write ten lines about bees or engineers or waitresses who
work three shifts or mothers with colicky infants who do not
sleep, or my friends who worse than these dash dollardly from
job to job. I sat broke all summer under a mango tree in Israel
and wrote and gardened a bit for food and sold old jewelry for
meat. Friends found me always ready for talk or love. Oh, there
have been flurries of busyness — at the computer company I
made databases and sometimes there were hours without time,
or student work piles up, or tax forms are due and overdue,
and the hive's cells are empty and winter is coming and no one
else is working so I do, but not for long. Today, for instance. I
watch my colleagues work, and they — well — maybe they are
peeking at me here and think I'm working. Clouds write slow
odes against the sky, pale gray on blue, so hard to read I stop
and write myself but write slower than the clouds. My heart is
fast and runs around my ribs like my daughter's hamster in its
wheel, and memory works harder yet and constructs my life
in configurations changed every time I stop thinking, which is
often. Last night, I heard Gil Shaham play the Beethoven violin
concerto, and I did not move even once and my heart slowed and
memory stopped, the way they did when I met Susann or ate the
first ripe mango or saw portulacas I'd scattered on the sand — red,
orange, yellow, pink and everywhere.

Deep in Thought

At 2 AM he sat, his wife asleep,
his animals and children long asleep,
and read what poets and philosophers
had written in their studies late at night
of lust, the body's life outside the brain,
outside of life and thought, and was convinced
that yes, the feel of flesh, the stroke of skin
on membrane, loss of I, the death of self
in other's complimentary loss of self
was better than his tortuous working out
of pattern. He had much skill at such abstract
concluding. The dog and children stretched
and smiled their dreams; his wife, turning alone,
her bedclothes crumpled on her rumpled bed, groaned.

FACULTY MEETING

"Hot and cold are just relative terms"
(like aunt and uncle and third
kissing cousin — I always liked
lovely sick Rosanne — removed by force.
hurled screaming into a state
mental hospital) a physics teacher
working next to me
intones inanely.

Hot candle snot
dripped across the plastic
cover of velvet table pads,
stains of Beaujolais nouveau
like seed shoots spread
or had spread early
as sun's alarm clock
before drear friends broke day
they watched blue light
yellow through red to black.

We should kill the children.
We should get divorced.
Maybe we should clean up
instead.

Etherize me. Patient.

Cold as fever. Ice snags my head.
A dead lover's knee in a winter bed.
Roseanne's?

Home is not on fire
exactly and I could go there
squirting lighter fluid marked
for domestic use only.

Do Not Eat the Pangolin

*It is theorized that novel coronavirus was released into the human
world by people in China eating pangolins. So:*

The pangolin, the scaly headed beast
eats crawling ants and termites, toothless,
licking up its prey with its sticky tongue,
busy and mindless as a scholar gathering
ancient comments on a language long
safely and harmless, gone, sucking up his lunch.
Poked with a stick, he can rise up and though
he cannot bite, he can somehow infect
the universal library. Leave him alone.

FOR THE ISRAELI ASSOCIATION OF WRITERS OF ENGLISH

Probably I am the best poet-in-English
in the State of Israel and as a friend said
that is like being the best poet-
in-Sanskrit in all of South Florida
except that South Florida may be
bigger and there is something exotic
about Sanskrit. Try to imagine being
the best poet-in-Mongol in Russia
after the Mongols left or the best
harpooner-of-whales at a meeting of
Friends of the Earth! Here I am performing
like a growling man lost among wolves, or if
that is too harsh, say that I grow
like a rare, rank weed in a field
plowed for a different crop.

Globalization

I am wearing a cotton shirt woven in India
and next to it in my closet was another cotton shirt a Scottish
plaid, woven in Saudi Arabia by people I hope
aren't Islamic terrorists, but it doesn't matter
and in a rack above is a silk shirt from the Mariana Islands
and some blends from Costa Rica and one from
The Former Yugoslavian Republic of Macedonia.
Some shirts are made in America, by Kenneth Koch, I think
or Lawrence Ferlinghetti, or a tailor from South Street
in Philadelphia. Most countries send me shirts
except Italy and France, which are too expensive.

My pantry, too, dissolves boundaries. Chutney and soy sauce
and coffee — coffee! — Kenya, Columbia, Sumatra,
Guatemala, Honduras, Jamaica, Hawaii, Yemen,
Ethiopia, Mexico, El Salvador — even Zimbabwe
which contributes nothing else — and Costa Rica.

Wearing a Kenneth Koch shirt, I pour a cup
of Columbian coffee. A beautiful Swedish woman
adds cream and we watch the red leaves of the Japanese maple
as we stir in contraband Cuban sugar brought to us
by a Canadian friend before I stride off in my Spanish shoes.

GOD MUST HAVE HAD A REASON
FOR CREATING MOSQUITOS

A green hammock on a green lawn
pink peonies and yellow iris,
iced wine and clean paper
and all afternoon. So pleasant,
so deadly.
In Lethe, but lovely, living.
So easy to fall asleep.
Mosquitos must be insects
sacred to the muses.

Still, I would settle for this,
right now, forever. This is a forever
afternoon. For when the ice
melts, and the paper's full
as these damned biters' bellies,
I will be going inside.

HEART TRANSPLANT IN SUID AFRIKA

"Go see what the doctor wants,
Charlie," chuckled the dying despot
to an athletic aide.

The Social Register and Who's Who
unlisted Samuel Smith whose nerve
graft (in his left leg) left him less
than half the man who'd filled the forms
out. After the false teeth, new corneas,
a young girl's liver, Reverend
Adam's soul, his psychiatrist's brain,
skin swatches and hair switches,
and his wife Matilda's poor drowned heart,
Sam was fifty-two per cent buried
at an average age of a hundred ten.
"Please, son, you've got to help me."
"Who are you, tattered old woman?"
"I am your kidney's mother."
Spirits crowded beneath lit windows
colorlessly intone
desire for old organs. Fights
will mark the resurrection of the dead.

"HYPOCRITE PERFECT — HOPING I ENDURE"

Berryman Sonnet 110

"Let passion burn" but who's to be the flame
and who the tinder? I'll be burned out and you
ashes. Or, you be brief and lovely, I'll
be dark and last. Yet why be perfect?
A smaller heat, a glaze — whispers instead
of searing cries, a smaller truer love
that hurts a little for a little while
but we'd both limp away, and may be back.

It wouldn't work. People are too dry
not to blaze up at matches — who needs torch —
or will explode like bombs, nudged the wrong way.
They want to be! To feel their faces flare,
their minds and bodies melt so instantly —
they think they will get up again. Some do,
their histories gone, their homes; let priests and children
whimper, no one's here. Once, both were perfect.

IMMORTALITY

For Frank Meyer

The Gourmet Cookbook drools
over Meyer lemons, writes "a cult has developed"
adoring them, these crosses of sweet orange, lemon, and
"a touch of lime." Meyer lemons are scarce,
and sweetly and tartly delicious
like nights wrapped in the arms
of beautiful women, crossed with grand opera
and a touch of mathematical genius.
You will not find Meyer lemons in Stop and Shop.

The eponymous Meyer vanished "mysteriously"
from a river boat laden with lemons,
plying the Yangtze Kiang in 1918.
I think he was thrown overboard
for obvious virtuous reasons.
The fruit was banned in America until the 1980s
(by then we'd let in anything). If you find
Meyer lemons, use them or preserve them;
they can't be stored fresh,
as kisses cannot, or frozen
like childhood.

In my refrigerator, sealed,
is a quart of Meyer lemons.
I will not tell you how I got them.
I cut wedges from some, salted them, added
the juice of other Meyer lemons, poured

extra virgin olive oil on top
and sealed them. I have not
eaten any, but licked my fingers
as I worked. I smiled for two days,
and my mind loved me
for the first time in years.

Susann pounds twenty spices for *ras al-hanout.*
I shall compose a lamb tagine.
We shall serve it with rice
and preserved Meyer lemons.

Iowa, Early Spring

After reading one too many road-kill poems

Early evening, a very few returning birds
sang vespers. On the road, emptiness, my headlights
focused on nothing as new nature
disappeared. Near Coralville, a bicycle
stumbling, drunk perhaps, out of the almost dark
fell into the cone of light
like a flaw in creation, a discontinuity
in my even lines, a jar in thought,
blood and jagged bones. He gasped and moaned
gasp, gasp moan, gasp moan
moan moan gasp moan..
The meter seized me as the rhythm of death
so suddenly sprung. The poet breathed a little more
then stopped, beginning the long caesura.
I pulled him off the road and fixed his words,
laid him beneath a birch that waited there
in tangled roots, wet leaves and paper waste
thrown out of cars, next to the longer dead
raccoons and rabbits, lamented by many a passerby,
and drove away, full night now,
knowledgeless, except for owl cry.

KITSCH

*On being told my choice of work to read at the New Jewish High
School's Arts Festival was inappropriate*

Anger and the joy of being heard
even misheard I wrote and read
"blue panties" and I deeply hurt
a parent with a degree from Radcliffe
(I wrote and read "ass" also,
but that got by I guess).

The Cambridge ladies who live in furnished souls
come quick to thought.
Nothing has more retarded the advancement
of learning than the desperation of vulgar minds
to ridicule and vilify
what they cannot understand.
said Dr. Johnson, or should have.
And justice Holmes held most judicially that
one man's vulgarity is another's lyric.

> "Senator Smoot (Republican, Ut.)
> Is planning a ban on smut
> Oh rooti-ti-toot for Smoot of Ut.
> And his reverent occiput.
> Smite. Smoot, smite for Ut.,
> Grit your molars and do your dut.,
> Gird up your I--ns,
> Smite h-p and th-gh,
> We'll all be Kansas
> By and By"

doggerelled Ogden Nash.

LATER

I will get out of me
or open wide
to let you all inside.
Male or female, doesn't matter
which, seed or fertile
ground. Now, I'm pebble
on a rock, no rain
nor love will work me,
though a wind may
rattle me around, may,
howling like a god and strong,
hurtle me towards you. Duck.

MANIC EXUBERANCE

"Your poetry used to be manically exuberant"

I sailed drunk and sexy, dove and drove
in shades of apricot, odors of shit and lilacs
rough and smooth. Ten thousand weeds
were single and had names I told
you once, holding hands
in a green lot's splendor.
The bets were large
I sometimes won the losses
I always paid. I wallowed
where I would.

Austere this countryside and few
its flowers, cultured in rows arranged
weedlessly, wordlessly
like books read and reshelved.
Carefully the pruned rose spreads
exactly where I will. Rocks
interrupt the hillside. I kneel
and hardly rise.

My Students: Failing

Their futures on their faces
fade when no miracle
splits my grade book
to let them pass
and mercy ends
in, "I'm really sorry."
I am ashamed
of my own tears
poured like house whiskey
the nights before
I searched the meaning
of incomprehension
and cursed them, failures.

A gnome hoarding
grades like money,
I dance on parents' hopes
and like some minor god
condemn and bless.

Effort never counts —
not theirs not mine,
except we love, and then
only effort. Those grades
count more, but these
are taken to the bank.

Their looks say if you love me

let me climb. My look
is downcast as they fall.

In spring, I'll pull the four-year tulips,
prune the lilacs
to make them bloom.
There are whole years I've failed,
and once — a decade, but not courses,
and I've failed myself,
scratched the red mark in me
alone, and crawled off snarling.

Obsessive Compulsive

Bodily illness is something the patient has, whereas mental illness is really something he is or does... Actually, we use the terms "neurotic" and "psychotic" (and other psychiatric diagnostic terms) to characterize persons, not to name diseases.

Thomas Szasz

And much of what passes for imagination is only obsession, which is another kind of productivity, giving you what you want again and again and again.

James Richardson

Witch women up the block each Tuesday noon,
buckets of paint, two brushes turpentined,
looked porchwards up their four stone steps and knelt
to color over last week's work, turned red
to green or differently inspired sprayed
textures on the plain, the monohued
remains of Tuesday past.

           Across the alley
from my sisters' room a boy, about my age.
dropped marbles from an upstairs window down
into the grass or snow then ran downstairs
to gather all into a jar and climb and drop
them one by one again, hours on end.

A woman and her daughter on the balcony
of a small house in Ramat Gan shake cloths
in air and go inside and come back out
with different cloths. The hours pass. the women
chat, two minutes to a square of cotton,
sheet or shirt, synthetic table cover
or whatever can be waved. Once I watched
and timed a sequence. Every two hours
each piece of fabric shook its moments.

I'm trying not to write this poem. I've written
hundreds already, most of them the same,
with different colors sometimes, textures, new
trim. I drop them silently. I wave them
waiting for the wave back, for the salute.

Mickey Vaporized

An asteroid large enough to demolish a city the size of
Orlando passed within 288,000 miles of Earth without
being noticed by astronomers until four days later.

Wired, March 21, 2002

Or Famagusta, Haifa, Valparaiso,
but perhaps the destruction of those important
urban centers also might go unnoticed
(by astronomers) until four days later.

I love the science blurbs on Yahoo! — the unconscious
nastiness. Somewhere sits a science writer
imagining Disney World as concave lining
of a mile deep crater. Perhaps his folks
couldn't afford the vacation that
his friends' parents could,
maybe he hates the movies, or was molested
by some geek in a Goofy suit.

Or, maybe she lives in Orlando, his ex-wife
and that son of a bitch. Next time I deserve
the right to name the city. I sure know
where I'd have that rock fall.

ON THE DEATH OF ADDWAITA, A TWO HUNDRED FIFTY YEAR OLD ALDABRA TORTOISE

The last hundred years were strange. Everything
there was to know, I knew; still,
two hundred fifty-one appealed, the slow
waddle across the tank for the eight
hundred thousandth day, the same greens,
the tropical scummy water. There are
nine kinds of rain; I have known each a hundred times
and wanted to know more, or at least again.
Back and forth was my life. Forward and forward
ends too quickly, before knowing.

RIBS ON THE GRILL OUTSIDE

Ribs on the grill outside
and coleslaw, beer, hot pasta.
Ninety-six degrees, the children splash
from wading pool to sprinkler;
fat spits on coals, sweat streams
and water beads.

I'm doing this again, but better.

Fifty years old, and finally
or finally so far, I've got
the right wife and children
a job I care about
and the small brick house
is ours and my daughter shouts
"Wolf-proof!" She's six.

Under viburnum and in thick
sycamore shade impatiens bloom
pale and deeper pink. My young wife
tans on a sunny island
in a sea of shadows.

My son is three and does not remember much.
Marsha Pomerantz, who writes good poetry
about Lucy, an early hominid whose bones
foretell us, perhaps, said
You really did it, didn't you,
got away and did it right.

We're only your mistakes
aren't we? my daughter wrote
and I wrote back not only.

REVELATION

*More than a million revelers in Times Square cheered
as the giant crystal ball made its 100th drop and a ton
of confetti rained down on the urban canyon, ushering
in the new year."*

Associated Press, January 1, 2008

I do not remember ever reveling,
New Years or not. I've watched on television,
drunk liquor, kissed, but what is reveling?
What are a million people? "Jennelle Joset
and her mother, Wanda Bowers,
had been standing around since 1 PM,
wearing hats with big plastic wheels of cheese…"
I guess they were reveling. All over the world
people reveled, even here, in Israel,
where it is a work day, a certain light
reveling is reported. I suspect my children,
grown, reveled for an hour or so. I slept.
At 2 AM I woke to pee, looked at my watch,
and turned to kiss my sleeping wife. Whee.
"'It's a party city, it's wild out here!'
said Stephanie Smith, 21, of West Covina,
California, as her friends polished
off yard-long margaritas." Last night I drank
two whiskies and wine with dinner. I read
and talked and wrote. Sometimes I wish
I knew how to revel, but it's too late. Soon
I'll be sixty-eight, unreveled, always only me.

Safari

Last time I saw two lions that some rude
stonemason chipped, deep in the middle Bronx
in front of the house where I grew up
they were covered with information, like
BLACK IS BEAUTIFUL and CAROLINE SUCKS.
When I was young they were all gray and mute,
black was a color, Caroline unborn,
probably. All four ears are gone, trophies
for some descendant of lion hunters.
The badly carved more-man-than-lion eyes
have red paint splashed around and garbage fills
the space between the beasts where stairs begin
upwards towards the house, which is reverted
to jungle, and I become aware that I
have never lived here, and resheathe, easing
cautiously away, memory's big game gun.

Shunday (a lame gazelle)

Whence the gazelle droppings on my feet?
The scrape of leather on the concrete street?

I contemplate formality of verse
my teachers shunned and pour my whisky neat.

My height hurts. I imp along
immoral midways. Goodass jazz
sends Chivas down my stein.

My fright skirts pimpsong
streets, immortal musings —
send me your fears.

A grief history of time:
Tick tock tick tock
Tick tock tick tock tick tock
Ticktockticktockticktockticktockticktock
Hummmmmmmmmmmmmm.

Today is the forty-second day
of the counting of the omer,
the period between Passover and Pentecost
(see Deuteronomy) and I have counted.

Gazelle's leap, ghazals steep
verse in dada doodoo.

A lame gazelle is guzzling dirty water
from a muse's broken fountain.
His muzzle drips dark wet
on muddy grass I walk across later.

Shelley-Shallying

For Sean Singer

Poets are the unacknowledged pro bono
defense attorneys of mankind.
They are also, of course, the prosecutors,
pro malo. Some try to judge. Their readers
are the jury but sometimes
it's hard to find twelve. The laws themselves
are old and indefinite. They whirl
in autumn winds, are ripped by thorns
and crumble easily when interpreted.

Except for Wallace Stevens, have any
lawyers been real poets? Doctors abound
and now teachers at universities.
Legislators are terrible poets
like a lot of other poets and poets
pass laws no one ever hears about
but which many people obey.

THE GORILLAS AT MILWAUKEE'S ZOO

screw
usually near closing time.
Babies in rented prams,
walking children, shaking loose
a bored parental hand,
and parents, too, and teenagers
with arms ritually entwined,
all stop,
engrossed
when big black hairy arms
caress hairy backs and legs.
and they do kiss,
or at least rub their faces together.

Then he mounts her.
And, "Oh my God!"
And, "Come on, Jeanie!
Let's go see the birds."
Or people just quickly walk away
and only we are left,
and they, of course, but they
don't mind. Their eyes
are closed to make
deep raining jungles
and heaps of damp, warm leaves.
Afterwards, she cleans him
with her mouth. They embrace and go
back to their iron swings.

THE WAGTAIL

After he pops
the wagtail, when he stops,
bobs tail feathers up
and down and up.
Makes a perfectly balanced
fool of himself.
Me too.
It's that or drop.

Tone Deaf Musical Notes

A pangolin with a mandolin in a daydream
once I was, rasping
of good Mount Moore.

A bird in the band
is worth two tubas.

Just move your lips, Eddie,
my teachers warned
from third grade on
abandoning my double bass,
but only I knew all the words.

Friends sing in choirs
or chant well prayers
I better understand.

"There are no wrong notes in jazz,"
Sean Singer (sic) tells me.
"The next note redeems
the one before."
Not my notes, pal.

Music falsifies, I comfort me,
distorts the clarity
of meaning's sweet concerto.

Where I've Worked, What I've Done

"Our lives are divided into work and eroticism."
Georges Battailles, *Death and Sensuality*

In childhood, I
mowed lawns
shoveled snow
sold greeting cards and magazines
    door-to-door
collected deposit bottles
cleaned out basements for their paper and metal scrap.

In and just after high school I
drove an ice cream truck (Sandra)
canvassed for a furnace cleaning scam
was a para-cop in a corrupt city
    pointlessly counting cars for money
caddied (Susan)
distributed free samples
    of Mister Clean
bused tables (Rita)
bell-hopped.

While at college and university I
unloaded trucks (Tina)
delivered mail
tutored calculus (Margo)
sold men's clothing in Greenwich Village
    (Peggy, Elaine, Barbara)
sold toys at Bloomingdale's (Maria)

waited tables at the college dining hall
    (Martha, Penny)
was a statistician in a slaughter house
    in Cedar Rapids, Iowa (Cynthia).
And then, I
taught writing and literature at colleges
    (Karen, Ronitte, Shelly)
taught high school English in Israel
copy-wrote
technical wrote
poetry wrote
translated Hebrew to English
    for the Israeli government
    for poets
    for many companies
analyzed data bases
analyzed business and communications systems
    for computerization.

Now, mostly, I
teach Jewish History, English, writing
    in a Jewish high school.
    (Susann)

Or I could start on the other half
though there's more work than women.

TOOTHPICKS

A physics assignment: Build a bridge using nothing but glue and two boxes (forty grams) of toothpicks. It must show a high weight-to-support ratio.

This poem is a bridge built of toothpicks
held together by good Elmer's wood glue
clumsily applied. A man could drive
a big truck loaded with centuries across
this bridge. This bridge weighs less than forty grams
including ink and paper and brownish ooze.

I walk across my bridge supported by
equations and ideas my hundred pounds
don't buckle or embarrass. On girders
lights shine. Beneath them waters flow and fish
leap near the pilings. An Argo full of heroes
sails slowly and forever underneath.
This will last longer than the Golden Gate
the Verrazanoes and the bridge of fate
or my classmates' clever tricks with toothpicks.

APOLLO 11

With all the care and many times
the knowledge of those sky-seekers who
comprehended and up-built
Chartres and Notre Dame,
and at comparable cost, considering
inflation and changed rates of exchange,
we have devised — American genius —
a disposable cathedral
that can be duplicated,
at similar expense, to prove our piety,
and which — match this, ye ancients — flies.

AT LONG LAST, A GLIMPSE
OF A BLACK HOLE

Report in the New York Times, *April, 2019*

I love astrophysics, the mathematics
preceding observation, predicting
or maybe creating what we see.
I squint into the center of a calla
still growing, attached to a real stem
coming out of a real corm and root.
The center is dark enough in the sun
and disappears into the waning moon.

CONTRA NATURAM

"Annihilating all that's made..."
Andrew Marvell

We sit on folding chairs, white wineglasses
still chill in the summer sun, refilled
while children listen to Schumann playing
from the Shed at Tanglewood. The dry grass
is green and damp from sprinklers; July green trees
rustle, I think, in time as much to music
as to wind. A bird quartet is silenced
by the strings. We drive home slowly
through the hills, the green spilling down slopes
we watch pass backwards through the cool
air inside. Tomorrow in the garden,
sweating, bitten, we shall paint in red
annuals and hard trimmed coreopsis —
a picture for the window picture frame.

Divorce

After I'd published my wife's diary,
the one in which she confesses all, in
very bad prose, but spicy, detailed, full
of truly vile behavior, mixed with
accusations against me, only some
of them true, and after I had caused her
considerable pain, really, and been
kicked in the balls a few times (she knows where
it hurts, after all those years — I'd be
a fool to tell you how she did it) I
felt a lot better. For once I've done it
right, finished something, kicked the corpse and danced
on the grave of love, and am unrepentant
although I have no plans to do it again.

DIVORCE 2

After the divorce, I shall clear the nettles
out of the calendulas. When the papers
are finally signed, I shall answer the letters
that have heaped up. As soon as the children
are resettled, the words, too, will be freer
than they have been these past four years, and I
will recomplicate them, it will be harder
to know what I mean, but I will mean more.

In my weedy garden, the flowers gasp
and wait for my hands. Friends and family
are hurt; they have stopped asking about me.
My work cringes under my awkwardness
wondering when it can dance again. Soon,
I tell them all — when it's finally done.

Don't Breathe on Me

read our new flags, snakeless,
perhaps a blowsy blonde
bent towards a would-be beau
with arms held out palms out
in terror. The government decrees
six feet of separation man from man
and man from woman. What Kama Sutra
diagram or picture offers ease
when fear of death makes sex impossible
to resist? My gardener weeds flower beds, the flowers
scent amorous air. To mock us bees
stroke pistils softly, pat pollen in
that deathless dark and yearning female place.

FOR (OR AGAINST) DONALD TRUMP

His lies, those emblems of commerce,
as normally false as any ad for margarine
that falsification, and his scorn for weakness
like a commercial for four-wheel drive SUVs,
fit into the surprised, unpromised richness
sprawling drugged from sea to polluted sea
while injured eagles flap the mountains
trash strewn, riddled by infected streams,
eggs thin shelled by insecticide. He is
America. It would be false to vote
for anyone else, some democratic poseur.

I Will Arise Now ...

I sold the children first, one at a time
and the house, room by room. Ties and jackets,
the furniture, most of the books and a lot
of years I just abandoned, tossed away,
dumped into puddles nastily, melted down
the rings and bracelets for the gold and sold
that too and with the cash jammed in my pocket
barefoot shambled to town, while my head cleared.
And there were grinning children and fine houses,
clothes my size, volumes of new verse and stories
not too often used, all dry or drying.
I bought a calendar, amiable brats,
a cottage and some baubles, filled my shelves,
and I live here now, satisfied at last.

It Is Hard to Keep Score

Dropped by their Saudi brothers
our USA-constructed bombs have killed
over a hundred Saudi fighters caught
by Houthi rebels. Why do I think
there is a poem in that? "Houthi" sounds comical.
Or imagine gray-black prison stone
decorating a solid wall with red and brain-gray gore
of captives awaiting torture, muscles torn
tendon and sinew apart, hands lopped
not so neatly off, the staged scene
a sense-filling entirety, nothing left out,
the scent of terror-shit and bloody copper,
my pain imagined in my reading. Saudis and Houthis
equal in their hating of us Jews
and so no side to root for
except us humans, just a few of us.

The Return of Comet Ikeya-Zhang

Experts believe this is the same unnamed comet as one recorded in 1651, meaning it is returning after a 341-year orbit. One Japanese newspaper announced Ikeya's find under the headline, "Could it be the same comet seen by the samurai lords?"
                              Associated Press, March 15, 2002

And by a Jewish farmer near Safed
who attended mystic sermons and ecstatic
midnight prayers. Almost certainly by
Siberian reindeer hunters and herders
and by some North American Indians
dying of measles and whooping cough.

Ice and dust refracting and reflecting
sunlight and time. A long count calendar
of creation's overflow, waste, refuse,
pointless save the power of imagining
samurai lords, farmers in Galilee
musk oxen and dead Indians. My first
kiss happened in a park, at dusk, in Camden
New Jersey, and a bird, a crow I think,
cawed. When my first son was born, in Iowa,
Leonids burst a star snow between dark
clouds and darker thoughts. Since then crows have cawed
and meteors flashed, but no first kiss or son.

Ikeya-Zhang has a new name this time
around, and we new kisses and new sons.
Silk suited samurai stalk Tokyo now.
Mystics are sillier, Yakuts drive snow-
mobiles and Indians stay dead. This comet
never shone before, never will again.

Mother of Child Burned in a Terror Attack to the Terrorist on Trial for the Attack: "I hope your children burn"

I understand revenge. When Skylab fell
flaming from heaven, I prayed aloud
that it fall on my cruel ex-wife, thundering down
like the wrath of God, and when my sister sneered
refusing to repay a loan we made
from funds received in Deutsch Marks, compensation
for months in Nazi death camps, Susann's Mother's,
I wished at least a burning, although not
of nieces and a nephew. I have punched
three stitches worth of pain into a false
old friend, and disappeared some others
as thoroughly as fire wipes out forests.
These actions are not pleasant, no sweet revenge,
but necessary. We pursue justice. Justice.

TO A LADY – LEAVE TAKING

"Tell me not, sweet..."
Richard Lovelace

Just as the rusted hulk,
wheelless, its windows crazed,
its jagged edges hard to move around,
that hid the secret entry,
the one I used to use
into the garden,
finally was hauled away,
so has at last your bulk
been lifted from me
and all the thoughtless green
your body hid, opens again.

An Invitation from my Daughter to Spend Simchat Torah at their Yurt in Nechusha

I will be eighty soon
and my legs and back and some other parts
that once made me happy by working
do not work anymore, or nevermore
as Poe's Raven declaimed
and if I come to spend the holiday near your yurt
in a house you have arranged for me
because I cannot climb the stairs to your yurt
and I sleep on a lumpy sofa, I shall become
furniture, a clump of person visited
from time to time, during
the long hours of prayer. Old age
is better spent at home, with my dragons
and views of my garden, surrounded by
books and better memories of my youth
and Middle Ages. It is not lack of love.
I most respectfully decline, a bee too old to reach a rose
or an old Phoenix, missing his fire.

ARS POETICA

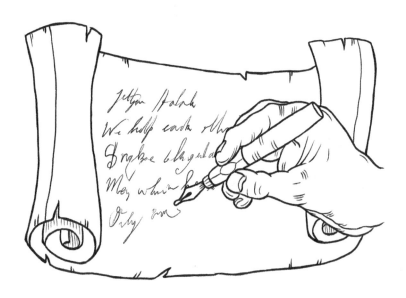

AFTER A POETRY READING, I WALK IN THE GARDEN

An old woman, a mediocre poet
reads in the present tense of making love
a lover opens her blue shirt to kiss
her wrinkled breasts and I walk under
the ancient olive tree, drops of sweet oil
drip from the split black fruit.

Lifescape

This is a lifescape I painted
to escape from life, preferring to pretend
to come to grips with the ungrippable
rather than to play with its fringes
like a scientist, or a landscape painter.

The bottom is all white
(original sin is invisible in an infant)
and without texture. Above this
are loops and swirls of Oedipal gray,
desire doomed to unfulfillment,
and then the muddy green, all blotchy,
of early spring. Greens darken into emerald
and the surface flattens into death
when, spouses chosen and children born,
all functions have been performed.
Then a broad band of black.

The top half is all black, except, to include
those who are hurt back to life,
I placed a triangle of color in the upper
left hand part of the blackness. Here,
after the somber gray of reawakening,
I painted the summer greens that come
with unforced choices, post-sordid freedom,
and the yellow, mellowing to orange and red,
of beloved transitory accomplishments.
There are darker patches in this bright figure.

At the top is the almost black of the earth
At midnight.
The frame is richest
walnut, ornamentally carved only enough
to emphasize the fineness of the grain.
I have painted it blue.

A LARGE ABELIA GRANDIFLORA

I don't dislike it, but there are problems.
The poems in Poetry (Chicago) rarely
make any sense, read them as often as you like.
I want to cite some lines but not a one
stays in my mind. Little aesthetic nudges;
I'll look a poem up: "Gazelles" from Poetry
(Chicago) June this year, the poem starts:
"Morning wind-wind everywhere
water mouth dry-mouth-dry finish
g-a-z-e-l-l-e-s gazelles
hooves s-e-e-d-s there stuck.
Gazelles trot-trot
hooves s-e-e-d-s fall-away
grass meld-pillow protect."
And then adds a hundred lines that feel to me
like thousands, so I skip them. So do you
and almost everybody else.
I have been ill
For years, I stay in bed most days my pen
changed to a laptop, my garden thriving now
as my wife and gardener do my work.
Except for Oxycontin I can't get
up and about. I swallow pills before
I go outdoors and see the white Abelia
I planted years ago, before the rest
of my garden died, neglected. Like me
the bush is still alive. It is a poem
besides its sweet biology. Listen:

the bush, Chinese in origin, rises
seven feet above the irrigated
soil. White flowers cover most of the green
of its flourishing. Twelve years ago
I dug its planting hole, and many other
grasses, flowers and ferns and a mini-forest
and every day I weeded, until ill,
three years in bed until a pill with a bad rep
let me stand up. S-t-a-n-d u-p. Gazelles indeed.
One leaps into my garden, scaring lizards
and their dragon father. A phoenix falls.
Sunbirds iridesce, and a mythy sun
burns far above cloud wisps, telling time.

An Old Man Falls Down at Night

Last night I fell, walking the two short steps, really
a step and a half between the bathroom door
and the edge of my bed. Anapests, I thought
and lay still on the floor wondering if this was it
that a hip had broken, a stroke had disconnected
balance and desire. Some day I won't get up
but last night was not that someday
and I cursed and out of breath
pulled myself to my knees, yelled for help
and crawled and pulled and stretched and pushed
on the floor on the wall (anapests!)
until I lay stretched out and without breath
as a giant flounder landed, eyes still clear, scaly.

CHAYLEIGH DANCES

Out of the blood and gore,
past the spit-up, little shirts
smeared with crushed fruit
or much cooked grains,
pizza later, and party clothes
and reluctant beard-shy kisses —
this poem started well then fell
like every grandfather poem not about
a dead or dying child, or somehow death
like Hopkins' autumn leaves
or Ransom's Chucky — to sentimental crap,
a child-kissed beard. Well, a tutu,
music, little turning legs, an audience,
my ordinary love, and wild applause.

It Must Have Been

It must have been when our Jungian forebear
sat on a safe stone outcrop, or balanced
on a middle branch, belly full, one late
afternoon, and saw distances that were not
for hunting, that the trouble started. "Huh?"
he must have thought, and if he had no mate,
found one, or made fire; fought or took a friend
and mapped the strangeness into shelter and women.

NAMING STARS

(At the drive-in movie on a clear night.)

I know four constellations. I tell them
and we wave. For the rest,
I make up new arrangements, different
dotted lines. (Even lovers stare
as cloths clean the rear window;
what an awful movie. We turn down
the sound, to keep the baby sleeping.)
I know Orion, three star general
primitively armed, and Leo, fierce
guerilla of celestial swamps, and
both bears. The rest are points of light
and I am little better off than Adam,
who knew these things need names.

I consider a great zigzag
through them all, and just one word
to circumscribe all worlds. I try
but my lines cross, my ends won't come
together, and it would be
too difficult for children, anyway.

(There is bourbon in the back seat.
I take a paper-cupful, and wander off.)
It is not easy, naming stars.
No inspiration comes. An anti-muse
is in this bottle. What myths can I choose?
(A voice, then a long blonde head,

pretty but disheveled, angrily asks
what the fuck I'm doing
prowling around their car. Her friend
pulls her back, before I can explain.

At the refreshment stand, a girl
thirteen at most, leans forward to accept
her paid-for pizza.
Her starting breasts, her bright legs,
elate me. In the air, I swallow twice,
the whiskey, and follow her
back to the car, with my eyes
only. A boy half lifts her
inside.)
　　　Flowers perhaps.
Loops of stars like daisy petals;
the bears are tulips. Water-
lilies around the horizon; comets
and meteors as pollinizing bees
among dim parent planets.
(I return to my friends and family,
I hope she won't get pregnant.

Another cup to drink. On screen
a prairie wolf pursues a fast
young ostrich, I think it is,
in color, between movies.
Then many naked Swedes
ask questions in strange beds.
I know those answers;
I rise and walk around.)

The concave screen hides many stars.
(Beyond it lovers, without pretense
or without cars, perhaps,
surprise me.) I am no voyeur;
those stars can wait, or let
the lovers name them. I
have named none. Fragile flowers
after all, are not star-stuff.
Adam said, "It's a hippopotamus
because it looks like a hippopotamus
to me." I know too many words.
Ezekiel saw wheels, but he had help.

(The manager has tracked me down.
He requires my ticket stub,
escorts me to my car
and apologizes. My wife
and sons are in front. My friends
feel each other. Time is short. Close focused,
a girl masturbates unhappily.)

My groups must overlap, touch
each other to the third star in.
Let them be shapes without names,
but shapes, interpenetrating
as they move. And already
some have moved, in October,
and the show is over. (I drink deep
from the bottle as we leave.)

NAMING

According to the language of the place,
the language spoken by the place's poets,
the names are fixed, more or less forever,
and should be learned. As aid to memory
(there are so many names, so many things)
buttons could be put a child's reach high
on those things on the ground (trees come to mind)
attached to tape recorders and small speakers such
that gentle pressure might reveal "maple" or "palm'"
and passing by, another button pusher might hear "child".
No one need press a button to hear "button,"
inventions are first names and later things
unlike, say, rocks and robins. Robins fly
and fish are hard to reach, but problems here
are only technical, and can be therefore solved.
Last night I touched you barely and heard "love"
yet am unwired myself, although I speak
fluently, and push and press and stroke
the who and what around me for response;
or am I lost here, not knowing in what tongue
my naming is, or where I am, what place.

NO ONE READS POETRY ANYMORE

A university press recently received over 5,000 entries in a contest
for book length poetry manuscripts.
The winning entry, published, sold 300 copies.

So no one is reading this. I could stop —
I should stop. Concerti for the deaf,
caviar for tongue-numbs, single malt
for teetotalers. But relax! If no one
is reading this, it can be very bad:
worms, not caviar, rock and roll, rotgut.

Sort of like a lot of poetry
I've read lately. Scentless roses.
Faithless dogs. Streets
where no one walks and SUVs
scatter illiterate litter
to clogged gutters no one cleans.

I have stopped, almost. But
everyone is writing the poetry
that no one reads anymore. I'd hug
those three hundred people
if they weren't libraries, stocking
their lonely dusty shelves.

No One Reads Poetry Anymore, 2

Yesterday, twenty people read my poem
the one I wrote that day, in my steep decline
although the red flowering vine in its new pot
blossomed lasciviously barely waving
at a white butterfly jittering past
defining silence, announcing beauty.
Twenty people is a lot. They are almost
a classroom full, their bodies stretched
lifeless as a street in Gaza
after we have announced death from the air
noisy and noisome in the afternoon
in Mediterranean sunlight, barely under
a high white wisp of lacy cloud, that
would make a jaded dragon cry out sharply.

Scribbling

Where was the plague last year
when men died normally, of age
or war or hopelessness or self-
consuming rage? Now, tumbrils waver down
the reeking streets, a woman stumbles
bearing dead the child she bore alive.
Note the internal rhymes
and clever prosody. Poems don't die
not even bad ones, scan
bookstores and learned journals
and the internet. Poets may drop
their hands from laptop keys
their bottoms sliding floorward
their last line just barely
ending on a rhyme. Late Yeats or Stevens
and I rest my case. Oh yes the plague,
the horror like the fall, of Troy perhaps
or one last gas attack for Wilfred Owen.
How serious these deaths! How stark
the times before and after deviate.
And we are here as on a darkling plain,
corporals in an ignorant army
awaiting orders ready to attack
when reason shouts surrender I
limp with old age, I am so sorry.

The Composition of the Universe

*Dark matter is a form of matter thought to account for
approximately 85% of the matter in the universe and
about a quarter of its total energy density. The majority
of dark matter is thought to be non-baryonic in nature,
possibly being composed of some as-yet undiscovered sub-
atomic particles.*

Wikipedia on Dark Matter

A poem meant to encompass all that is, a footnote
to Einstein and Wallace Stevens, Notes Towards
a Supreme Fiction or a general theory
explaining everything, fails like a one ski jumper
in the Winter Olympics, because XXXXXXX
most of the snow has melted, eighty-five percent
run watery down, or like a baseball player swinging
with a toothpick bat. Xxxxxxxxxxxxxxxxxxxxxxxxxxxx
xxxxxxxxxxxxxxxxxxxxxxxxxxxxxxxxxxxxxxxxxxxxxxxxx
xxxxxxxxxxxxxxxxxxxxxxxxxxxxxxxxxxxxxxxxxxxxxxxxx.
In a poem, every x is an unknowable,
and represents much more of its
unknowable reality. Xxxxxxxxxxxxxxxxxx
I pretend, like Newton and even Heidegger
to know some things I haven't the vaguest idea of xxx
I am comforted by this lack of knowledge.
I know even less than fifteen percent
of the Bulbul's path through trees
and can't translate that sweet song.

I want to understand that little part
gleaming at the far edge of sight
and the scent of roses, the scent the bee smells,
not just this sweetness, red and aglow.

The Pain Against the Paper

Smash a car door on a thumb, catch
horror in a space that matters, watch
it ooze out, that instant, every instant,
between knowledge and scream.
Then apologize. Show how skilled
at cleaning wounds, bandaging,
comforting you are, how compassionate.
Walk your subject home, return, find
the poem in the blood, drying,
streaked on the side of the car.

Weather Report

Today I ignore the poems pushing their ways
through the green weedery, the white rose bush
climbing the lizard wall, the hedgehog terrace
where the crack of snail shells fills hedgehog throats
and pay no attention to the poems
floating a foot above the pages in *Poetry* and *The New Yorker*.
My left leg hurts a little at a time
and my left hip makes it impossible to sit down.
Today is prose, with a sprinkling of poetry on the horizon.

Yetzer Hara

Only snake writes, a soil sprung in my fingers,
teeth tearing in the dark of my breast
a tail flexing and relaxing around my legs
the sealed body around my gut
wound in the windings.

Sometimes snake sleeps
or sheds, in cold weather, while the rains
wash away hunger, when the children
play quietly and the light lies a little.

Sometimes
I wake up snake, before the peace
settles too thickly and my head aches
my hand lies like red leaves, not moving,
missing the rustle of snake.

I snicker and invite my snake.
My ears fill and empty with the hist! of snake.

Winter Painting Number One

For John Lobosco

The imagination is perverse, deep orange
when the eyes see white, pale blue
against a dead gray sky. Cold scribbles
on the window, spackles the walls.
The canvas is on fire! Red and orange flames
spread out and up, so warm the hothouse
of the mind-forced green lies
over the almost middle, and springs
forcefully.

Imagination twists us happy
falsely and well, makes diamonds out of glass,
a longing smile from cool politeness.
We walk through ice on grass,
hands intertwined, our green-gray eyes
aflame, bejeweled and dazzling.

Our world is warm, John, and nature cold.

Winter Painting Number Two

For John Lobosco

> *Reality is only the base, but it is the base.*
> Wallace Stevens

Sticks of imagination flare and fade
and through dispersing smoke the mud,
frozen, and still some petrified green
bereft of life-force, shudders through dirty snow.

Desire pokes the ashes, orange sparks,
yellow, red, ages' creations
mimic the manic speculations
of summer, that hot bravado.

Blue patches are illuminated. They illumine.
I write in May, imagine you imagining
winter again, cold burning in your head
and mine. Yellow forsythia, tulips,
 pink weeping cherry hover
over the chartreuse lawn. I shiver
at the hard mud, the gray snow,
and stand stunned in the almost warm of now.

WINTER PAINTING NUMBER THREE

For John Lobosco

> *One must have a mind of winter*
> *And have been cold a long time...*
> Wallace Stevens

Now the canvas shrinks and figures
condense, compress. A red star rises
in borealic sky, the coldest fire.
Tinderless, the imagination
curls without comfort in a chilled desert,
a moon of Saturn free of mind-melt.

The universe is a Neolithic cave,
commanding color, that vaulted cavern
an empty skull, its fleshless inside daubed
gray, pink, green — blue glows in sockets.
Nothing will warm this beauty
before creation, so deep in winter
memory soothes no spring, no fall
from skull to cave to empty heaven.

Winter Painting Number Four

For John Lobosco

> *Mid-winter spring is its own season...*
> T.S. Eliot

Mud melts and lies above the hard months gone
and yet to come. Lichen paints life
on exposed rock, gray-black through snow, twilight-
cleaned, covering less, oozing a little
as if the scab of winter were scraped off
and the raw flesh of the real earth is bared.

The blue imagination covers now
almost the sky, darkly and brightly.
Desire gathers yellow underneath
and almost warms the February mix
of hope and falseness. This painting is too true,
John, too much reveals the twisting, the mind's
lies, how intellect denies the presentness
of the great disorder. There are red wounds
like claw marks up and around as if torn
through the canvas back. I see they are.

Chaos behind and, in my mind, chaos.
In yours, too, I think, chaos is color
and shape and time, everywhere but the point
of paint and cloth, words on the page, the body
focusing music, distilling noise to dance.

A lie lived becomes a kind of truth,
the real of imagining, where yellow
yearns and green impossibly speaks of life
in February. Fictions of winter
illuminate my spring and clasp my mind
either hard of gently; now, then, and deep.

A Tree in Beer Sheva

There is a tree both constant and consistent
in that I see it bloom in winter too,
not snow flowers, real pink (fringed white),
unimagined, except the whole be. Film it —
it will be as focused as the elms
in Iowa backyards, those empty urns
among snow-covered stubble thrusting up,
not holding, not full: simple patterns
fixing and arranging. This tree is
too over-full to parcel, and is
itself unfenced; this beginning
is of its lesser fruit a distant, distant smell.

The tamarisk is unimagined, it is seen
in synapses whose own roots and branches
can be X-rayed in moments of perception
(which is imagined, and the tamarisk in its seed
and the later rains). We lie together
actual as flesh, and afterwards we dream
before beginnings, wander in dry sand
where seas were, before the fern was wood,
before we went away; and wake and alter,
now water pours on leaves and down the *wadi*;
passing, we see the unimagined tree
with greener eves and nothing has been changed.

DECISIVE

My brain is no computer, but my dog's
uncluttered may be one, food, sleep and love
his variables, or the pigeons'
on my window ledge, add only height
and chicks to feed. A variable's not
uncertainty, like naked human doubt.
My keyboard needs a key for "I don't know,"
or maybe gray is green if just the sun
would rise more slowly, slower still, almost
a stop between at a nameless tint, a tinge
darker or perhaps less dark. Dogs and pigeons
do not decide; they know and knowing act.
People act too, we fire guns or we squeeze
green on a palette, or maybe white, or black.

FOR HART CRANE: "LEGEND"

"Daily life" seen clearly, can't be, for long
or you go crazy as Hart Crane, and can't
anyway be seen clearly by anyone
I know. Maybe it isn't there, maybe that's
why we plant flowers around, paint the walls,
reassure each other with our pats and touches
of affection. Did Hart Crane see that? What
did he see? I think I'll go inside my head
and be platonic. But then I'd have
to sleep alone, and appetite won't stop
to let me be ideal. I think if I don't think
I see better, even if I see unclear,
like my dog, his nose to the ground, his ears
up — but he, too, whimpers in his bed
and growls at nothing. "Realities plunge
in silence by …" Yes, and we should let them,
Hart, and shut up, look away, enjoy
this carnival, this cosmetician's dream,
the five-sense circus of cheap thrills we are
in "daily life," laughing together, sighing,
admiring the conjuries we conjure —
and letting the "realities" fall where they may.

For Master Rotlevi

*It appears that Rotlevi's loss to Teichmann... liberated
a depression in his mind... He was taken to a mental
sanitorium... and he has never been heard from since.*

Edward Lasker in Chess Secrets
I Learned from the Masters

On sunny days his mind is almost clear,
and through the crenellations horses seem
to move in even lines. The draymen
wander loosely over the oblong fields
all in the same drab shirts. The fields are all
the same drab green. He can watch for hours
without moving, without needing to move.

Spring is harder. Dark plowed patches
alternate with sprouted corn. The nags skip.
A little sap rises in the sprung brain
of the aging master, peeking at his watch,
trying to ignore the crosswise walk
of the foreman, the landowner's slow step
from the farmhouse. When his wife shouts
the workers start, and Rotlevi screams.

I think it's worth it, master. One game
as good as another, if the mind stretch
to be the mover, accept the time, take
the time to push a pretty order
cut of itself onto a scaled world,
and should it break, so, chaos has to win;
resign this game and suffer out the years.

...To a Green Thought
in a Green Shade

The willow drug in summer when the wind
erratically stirs and overhead
the sun has finished rising, works like this:
wake early
do your day
eat a good lunch.
Under a full grown willow
(burrow through trail of leaves)
near the trunk, lie on the ground
face up. Focus your eyes
on patterns in the breeze
until the patterns stop.
Slide over, feel the bulk
of wood against you.
New patterns will appear
and disappear. Good.
Where is the wind
coming or going? From you
or to you? It doesn't matter
if you shut your eyes
the green still waves, shadows
of twigs and leaflets still
derange and disarrange
what order was, and mind
is green and twiggy
erratically stirred
and you are willow, much

as you've always been
but never knew.
This is the work of willow tree
in summer in a light breeze, at noon.

The Middle Ages

His sword wasn't, exactly, rusty,
more unpolished, dull, except the blade
and point. An excellent weapon still,
the lack of glitter arguing hard use
without time off for cleaning. When it whirred
over his head, the sun skittered only
at the sharpness, outlined the usefulness,
the spirit of the thing. Body was just there
to hold the edge. In his old age, his arms
tired, his will to slash patterns in the air
gone, he'll make it gleam, burnish all the steel,
I think he'll plate the hilt, engrave his name
along the gutter where blood ran. Then,
maybe, he'll die and then, perhaps, will rust.

Whenas in Silks

We know better now. Herbert, I suppose
knew better then, and wasn't fooled by clothes
or even skin. Spenser composed
most of a book exposing the deceit
and also I know how appearance cheats
by boiling time to vapor. Andrew Marvell
argues the other side, says time is cruel
and evaporates anyway, so should be drunk
right up. Those "instant fires'" banked
cannot be used. His "Garden" is later.
The problem is, knowing's not enough,
at least not only from the inside out,
from the underwater rocks and slimy bottom
to the pale pool I see, shimmering
in early morning, the wind folding
ripples, as the sun starts to warm,
a little redder over where sharp tips
of stone that would, I guess, rend
a swimmer diving in, almost surfaced.
It's harder from the outside in
to judge the danger underneath the skin
frothing away, but mostly water's cool
and deep enough. That man drying himself
in the warm grass on the other shore
looks happy. We, wiser of course, are never sure.

White Bearded Dragon

"If God could suffer as we do
God too would grow old"
wrote Le He, a thousand years ago
more than a thousand, before he died,
at twenty-six, from "general dissipation."
Where Le He died a tree
jade green even in deep winter.
I rub my white hair
God does not groan or ache
like an old dragon
white beard and faded scales
only razor teeth and unbanked fire
dragon I leash and lead
with a chain of words and rhythms
a weak old reptile now
while God does not get old.

EPISTEMOLOGY

The real world sprawls and climbs around me
I open all my senses and my mind
recoils at too much green, too many shades
odor of scallion, rose, the purple sage
sounds of ten sorts of bird, bees, flies
cars swooshing by outside the tall stone wall.
A lizard watches, sniffs and listens like me
my mind shuts out most senses
to let me understand much less but better
what the lizard knows, and every lowly weed.

Writing About What I Know

In class...
There is a girl in row five wearing blue panties
the color of imagination
Coleridge wrote
I think and my ass hurts
from the unbending metal of the folding chair
so I will stand and write on the board
and stop staring up her legs
which is embarrassing. I know Augustine
asked, in his Confessions, "What do I love
when I love my God?" and I know
in the back wall the bricks cohere
each to each in mind forged manacles.

The trees outside this fourth floor window are red
and soon brown. The stained carpet tears.
I hear whispers. There is no smell at all.
Pathetically, the trees are angry
and innocent and write only
that the obscure sky will more appear
in blue white gray as leaves fall.

I think too much and write nothing
and do not know what I love.

But I do know what I love
and cannot write it. Useless advice.

Blue sky and underpants, write
imagination, leafless and ignorant.

WHY THERE WILL BE NO POEM TODAY

A poem flickers past my mind
a lightning bug on speed spotted Dalmatian
chased by cheetahs little boys with jars
glowing with captives everyone a poem
pleading for paper, blotches on beasts
confuse me. Jasmine scent and citrus
mix in the dark with sharp aromas
of Susann's kitchen, cinnamon
and garlic cloves, a roasting chicken
and the blue-violet trail of the escaping poem.

THE WEDDING POEM

WEDDING POEM

1

Here on the beach at Gaza all those years,
four instead of three, fade into sand
and dust that trickled loudly through our hands
on that great voyage to this our very fine
and final place. In this fourth spring the grass
roots deep as tree, the trees spread deepest green,
and the hut on the vast sea's shore stands firm,
constructed of *Frog's* timbers, salvaged from
her late and unlamented wreck. Among
our friends, who wide-eyed gathered round
the sight of sailors hurtled through the land
into their midst, welcoming if bemused,
we plant *Frog's* final flag and summer flowers,
order our storms to cease, and are obeyed.

2

And yet the wind that ruffles through the cloth
that is our wedding canopy and lifts
its corners upward straining like a sail,
reminds my mariner heart of harder days
and pride at all that *geste* returns, as if
Moses, barred from Canaan, great and sobbing
after he'd come to terms with banishment,
written the lines about the unknown tomb,
arranged himself for death and closed his book,
were suddenly reprieved and found himself

facing new tasks, their outcome all uncertain,
but willing to risk his fame and reputation,
desert won, in settled habitations,
which needn't be abandoned after taking.

3

But I grow solemn in comparisons;
enough that each day waking where we wake
we see above our huddled heads and all
around our walls the scars of winter wars
which graved themselves into *Frog's* soul so deep
nor paint nor time nor plaster ever can
hide how we came here. Lovely daughter's blood
seasons these planks, and the shadow of
beautiful friend keeps watch above the booze
in the kitchen closet. My parents' shades
who sailed with me through Hell are conjured right
into the beams above and my Gypsy love
walks in the garden when the nights are warm,
murmuring restless, rustling the leaves.

4

This May I've hauled my craft ashore to stay
in its home harbor, now designed for hot
summer which is always, and as a model
for young and middle-aged and even older
men and women who need to take to boats
when stars move badly in their skies, when water
runs useless off their land, when the pump of blood
is calendar not clock to bell the watches
searching new coasts, or wonders of the sea.
One arm holds Susann, the other hold a glass

which toasts tied *Frog*, entire in this song
although dismembered and reshaped in wood
and tapered steel and cloth which drapes and greets
dear friends and guests, and needn't gather breezes.

5

This is my song and voyaging except
this epilogue which has not happened yet
and which is Susann's too. No prophet I
nor tracer of the histories of other
people's arrivals, storm-tossed and wild eyed
to havens, although I have recorded
the easier tales of those who drowned or jumped
ship when dread of one more winter's rush
down intermittent stream's uncertainties
congealed their hearts and made them choose to wait
their lives out in the desert. Susann tells,
her great brown eyes all satisfied, of how
the barque she fashioned cunningly and alone
crashed here ashore, but that's a different poem.

6

When there come winter nights when winter rains
smash against our windows in a gale
that strains foundations, tears through tiles above
and makes us fear the very walls will split
and scatter splintered wood around this strand
they're raised upon, clear will be the wisdom
of a boat-built home, tried against worse than these
or any other trick of man or nature,
for here are timbers seasoned by four years
of god-beating storms, storms that rock and time

both broke and tore while these wooden planks
came through, though often cracked and in dire need
of time off for repairs, for cleaning up
clotted gore, dead crewmates, memories and tears.

7

But why consider storms. Tonight is all
music and wine and dance, a day released
from striving time in which sweet music's strains
and Bacchus's bottles and the foot's fleet steps
have heavy prices, which I've often paid,
but not so often enjoyed, as those here who
have sailed part way with me may testify
this night of swirling song and swirling wine
and swirling men and women who like gods,
some of whom we've met and others heard of,
are all immortal, from now until the dawn
returns us worldwards. This is our gift to you
who gather here: one night of agelessness
within your bodies, moving out of time.

8

The journey now is onward in the mind
which was all struggling arms and legs braced tight
against the *wadi*'s wiles. Will peace disturb
the comradeship of sailors and will sleep
come harder to the unexhausted? Dreams
of dragons aren't dragons long; waking
will slay them, and the admiring maiden
who hailed the hero red with dragon wounds
worn in her honor may grow bored the while

362

the hero toils on land and sings the past
by candlelight, evenings when work is done.
But I have heard the scaly beasts abound
inward also, and we two yet may fight
the blazing teeth, the straining hideous head.

9

Summer approaches, and the new turned soil
calls out for flower and the fruits of June
we plant tomorrow and in weeks to come.
The rainless time is on us, but this year
we need not wait for winter to go on,
having arrived and free to pour down rain
to fill our inner seas and let us float
stormlessly where we will or else stand still
and watch our land turn colors, red and green,
rainbows of what seeds dreamt in dormancy
while we were on our way. Now is the world
amaking, now in May, the wetness dried
outside, the seabed brain alluring
lovers to journey on in their unmoving.

10

So now turns meditation what was all
motion and rage, desperate action all
directed towards arriving at this place
we sprawl upon, feasting on fat cattle
and fine herbs offered victors shipborne home
there to lie back in memories and bed.
But so all song is meditated speech,
dance meditated walk, and poetry itself

a meditation on all these performed
deep in the soul and graven on a page
as aid in agile thought. Our very house
is meditated *Frog,* our garden Eden
worked by the mind out of the dance of weeds.

11

May all the spirits and the weather gods,
the goddesses who kissed us as we sailed,
or wished us onwards or entreated stay
a season sweet ashore to dally dreaming,
the *wadi* nymphs and demigods and even
the demons under desert dense in sand
who killed full many whom I've mourned and left
behind me in these books or wanted to,
be here tonight, to gnash their teeth or laugh
and cheer this journey's end. My enemies
may glory in my many scars, their depth
and unfading color; the kinder gods
may bring long glasses, and I'll pour myself.

12

If now we're to stay still or move within
the compass of this land we'll need to learn
how to turn lovely without sailing on
or wanting to. Susann a center in
spring flowers once stood swaying on both feet
all imperceptibly except I saw
the grass come graceful round her knees and fall
new green in waves away directionless
that sunbirds iridescent swooped upon
to pluck up for their homes, soft woven from

reeds and tufts, under the thorny branch
which blooms deep red all year. And I discerned
Susann in thought, her large eyes glazed like rain
washing the roots of scarlet flowering trees.

13

My friends have all been nomads like myself
wandering across seas and lands and twisting *wadis*
across and through the homes and habitations
of Abels, settled Saxons, *fellahin,*
looting their hearts and money, taking wives
and leaving fast before the lure of the place
unplundered, peaceful, full of changes all
revolving with the sun and coming back
ever to harvest, and to undried meat,
fresh bread and aged wine, could tempt them from
the joys of ravaging fame and making names
which spread yet farther than themselves
and set their bodies more than their victims' farms
ablaze. All these have died or wandered on.

14

My love of change, insistence on the beauty
of mutable man, his whims and violent acts,
his wavering loves and appetites I've sung
throughout my books, and added underneath
the price he pays in Hell for joyously
slashing the bonds he ties upon himself
in fear of faring forth. The time is come
for gesture's grandness to be circumscribed
and passed on to the overfond of staying
where they are, rather than where they will.

For Susann and myself, having arrived
at where desire led us in magnificent
circle out of the law and smiling bleeding
back to the law again, it's time to dance.

15

This is the dance for lovers after danger
and after all the tests and trials have passed,
of those who side with hoarding dragons and demons
and would imprison God Himself, Who moved
sword, cloud and flame through wilderness to find
the place He willed to build Himself a home
around His priest-born gold adorned craft,
sanctified in blood. My stanzas now
become the lovers circling, which had been
their path those desert years when death had meant
defeat and unfulfilment, are become
a choric song and celebration after
narrative is done and written down.
My book is closed, my tongue begins to sing.

Epithelamion

In the tatting of the lace
draped on Susann's dress
and in the widening of her eyes
in the curve of hair around her face
are figures fit for singers
fluenter than I. Beautiful
as Susann is, tonight I praise
courage before grace.

Rocks hurtled hard by old
religious sounding men
tore soul and bone
and hurt the woman sore
until she bent and picked
the sharp threat up again
and whistled back the stone
into their hearts and left
the worst one as if dead
widowed his wife and made
orphaned the evil brood
which hungry Hell may take,
and their descendants, too,
God make them few.

The woman armed with wit
and beauty is a foe
even the evilest
would well be wary of:
the inland ogres who
are nameless in this song
will find themselves erelong
the villains of a piece
crueler far than this;
vengeance be taken next
on neighbors' craning necks,
those whom her laughter wrought
jealous of happiness
so when the dragon came
they gave it Susann's name.
The ogres, worse than dead,
are forced to hum along
to tunes of Susann's blows

against them and their brothers;
next door the neighbor whines
behind her window blinds,
and mourns her daughter dressed
to be the dragon's bride.

Trained in tenderness
she found the armor cold,
the dragon slashing sword
heavy in her hand
which is all soft and meant
for stroking more than killing,
but bound the iron on,
and grasped the sharpened steel
and, in the flames he breathed,
searched out the scaly beast
all loathsome slimy green,
guardians set to keep
natural heat and green
out of ladies' lives,
and when the fanged mouth
hissed loudly sin and shame
Susann took careful aim
though singed by the fire
which scars will never fade
for they are dragon made
and thrust into the throat
slicing the subtle tongue,
breaking the sibilant teeth,
poison lathered, gleaming.
The nay-saying serpent fled
back to its hidden den
where it lies now ahealing

pondering with what wiles
and ill-meant dragon smiles,
it may in years to come
try to bind again
coils on escaped Susann.

Out of her armor stepping into day,
the oiled sword set aside, the half-healed wounds
in soft and summer clothes and youth enwrapped
and open to May winds that soothe yet shake
the battle-blistered skin and heart awake,
Susann comes forward all defenselessly:
this is the prize of heroines alone
complacent in their strength and beauty so
they dare reveal themselves in grace and glory,
dance in the world they've won, and dancing spin
a story, weave a future, whirl their limbs
as innocent children do, before the summer
the brave have plodded ugly panting through
dries up their nerves and drives them into shelters.

How formal may my celebration be
of beauty freed and courage justified?
This poem is public, even if I chat
a few lines here in passing, gathering
my thoughts and faculties, the battle done
I've sung in symbols — not to be obscure
but out of hope that if I interweaved
the brain-black terrors with the earth outside
my listener would see in the dazzling day
his night-time manacles and cut them off
to walk light legged. The poem is private, too,
in that it's meant to serve as talisman

for Susann and for me in time to come
should we forget not only she and I
but dragons also are immortal and
wake hungry, angry, and revengefully.
These symbols, reader, strange and mythical,
are allegory always understood
in the child-like, newly-gentled sun.

We step from here into the heat and glare
of our fourth summer, perhaps our first
real season in these fields, leaving behind
the mystic deeps and deserts where we found
the myths we've made to live by, entering
tall perennials, a world of giving birth
and staying still and nurturing. Our hands,
which held so well the mainbrace, sword and helm,
now hold each other, and we lean against
softness of flesh made strong in more heroic
but far less pleasant times. Tomorrow morning
we start to turn the soil so long ignored
and plan the place of flower which will bloom
year after year, changing in a pattern
predictable in rhythm, soft in tune
as Susann's voice at evening, blessing all
the multivariate, comprehended earth.

16

My stanzas murmur on, their modulations
gentler than summer clouds above the sea
seen from the shore, their intonations
subtle as the sunset the horizon
blends night and day in its last hint of red
shading to ocean's green where the still water

enters the night, shimmering green flecked black
leading the downfalling sky. Overcome,
the *wadi* flows inside me, not as blood
but rather part as song and part as great
vastness of mind, the place imagined where
I learned to sing shouting heroically
the melodies I now croon soothing soft,
measuring out my lines and treasured years.

17

These are the years after the death I died
in a far inland world in which the eye
hunted but could not see, in which the ear
sought profit in cacophonies but never
awaited passive song and even my tongue
wrapped around taste in avid hunger fit
only for greedy death afraid that each
pleasure is meted out by a stingy god
whose store is almost empty. This new time
is mine and measureless, my senses now
are summer, late and always, and my choice
unforced as any animal's, well fed
and satisfied with all he has, proclaiming
the joy of being, announcing that he is.

18

Acceptance after striving, leaning back
and opening through each other to new worlds
otherwise unknown is the fruit of love,
and may its odor shape and interfuse
and be all herbs and spices to the songs
that take the place, finally worn away,

of time and journeying. Memory itself
rests quiet in the almost stillness of
motion's end, the eddying deep pool
at the start and finish, quavering, of time.
Now we sit down, and all the passive senses,
not like a newborn child's, arranging order,
but like an angel's, bound in immortality
to the beautiful chaos, open and know.

SAILING PAST
GAZA

Poem at Sixty-seven

I

I understand nothing. I know a lot,
from the jasmine barely blooming now
in late October to the sweat stained pages
of my many thousand books, piled, sprawled, shelved
in patterns. Susann and our children seem to flourish.

And every instant: sounds, colors, words, scents, and probably
what has no name. Outside, the sprinkler nourishes the roses
kills the marguerite, my words at dinner
inform and misinform, and change lives
like slow tapeworms, or like dew.

I am going somewhere that has no name
except what I call it — Simble perhaps,
where there are rabid koalas that eat meat
but don't like it. They are dangerous, but I laugh
when they roll down hills.

My daughter is in New York, where there is no jasmine
in mid-October. She is five months with child.
When she returns, I shall remember what she looks like,
dark, swelling, smiling. It shall rain, November,
as if prayers were answered.

Many years ago, smart men looked at the moon
and now they have holes named after them,
my son tells me in a poem. I like the thought
of Ed's hole, on the dark side,
a place no one would look, would find me.

Last night, we ate dinner on a terrace
overlooking a beach on the Mediterranean.
A quarter moon rocked in the clouds.
The loud sound of water on sand disturbed
my lack of metaphor, my purest meanings.

II

My investment advisor calls me, tells me to buy
call options on Starbucks stock. I am embarrassed
that I understand her. Last night, Leviathan
thrashed his great tail and waves hurtled towards heaven.
That is a lie. Truth is Starbucks, and water on sand.

In Simble, no one dies, but only I
control admission. What would you give to live there?
The warm and waveless ocean, fruit you may name,
the great library and art gallery, somehow
the symphony, and, of course, koalas.

I've always laughed a lot, loud and unembarrassed
so that, a boy, I could be left in crowds
and always found. I still laugh loud, but only
with reason, koalas falling or contagion
from a child. I do not laugh as much.

There are clouds in the blue sky. Some nights ago
drops fell like words and dried unread on stone
or soaked into soil. They will be overwritten
soon, palimpsests, like ancient tombs or memories
that once meant something, perhaps.

The open market ruins all my senses.
The filters break in shouts and sweltering fruit,
the smells of fish and freshness, rot and sweet.

A young woman, scowling, grasps a pomegranate
bursting and round, red, seedful dear.

These are the pills I take: cholesterol,
blood pressure, depression, prostate, aspirin
and one whose purpose I forget. I feel great,
doctor, I lie. At night, sleepless,
I drink brandy or, good times, scotch.

III

I wake befuddled and my ship's ashore
and has been for a year. Moss decorates
the northly timbers, and the deck planks warp.
We have arrived! The shipwreck's on display —
admission includes a poem and a beer.

This is the house I plan to leave feet first
but not right now. The shrubs are overgrown,
the dog untrained, a promised essay
barely started — I have much to do,
two books to write. Perhaps next year

or later. For now, I conjure soup
of meat and pomegranates, cabbage, spice,
a few potatoes, lemon, coriander leaves.
Then tiny chicken breasts in orange liqueur
and Chardonnay from the Golan.

When poets visit, converse is of who
we are, and I never know what "we" is.
I am so many and all patterning is lies.
I cook and garden, write and love and pray
and think and read and look always at you.

I don't work anymore, no salary
trickles mildly in then gushes forth.
My pension's modest as a new sworn nun
and my habits cost more. This is not Chaucer
To His Purse, we manage, and so did he.

My sister's husband died some years ago
of prostate cancer. He was greedy, stupid,
stole, lied, bragged and died at last in two
wretched rooms disgraced. My sister loved him —
dumb bitch. We do not visit or telephone.

IV

I have a patch, black, on my left eye, and am tired
of pirate jokes. Were I a pirate, I would have
your gold, your women and your uncut
first editions of eighteenth century novels.
It would be fun to be a hairy pirate. Arrgh!

Who are these Israelis? Why can't they be
the people who live here? I live here. I am
as Israeli and a Simbilian and more.
I live on lumber and on polished teak,
smelling of rain forest, colors of macaws.

All that I know are words. What's a macaw
outside a zoo? My cage is syntax,
dictionaries, form pretending meaning,
where even God's a word to poke and parse,
love best expressed by probability.

Saturday morning, Susann set out at least
ten kinds of cheese, soft, hard, white, yellow,
blue tinged — blocks, rolls, wedges, and tubs.

We sipped good scotch and nibbled fancy bread.
The feast was offered prayerfully to God.

My son and I sit and revise his poems
about the moon. They are love poems, and sad
because he is twenty years old, and hurts
in mind and soul. Mine too are sad tonight —
but only body aches and that will stop.

Hundreds of poets send me lines to publish
in a magazine I edit. They know they hurt
but not in words. It is like getting notes,
strangely written, from dogs — instead of yowling
about their torn, bloody and broken legs.

V

Chicken breasts, sautéed in olive oil
on a bed of peppers, mushrooms, onions,
with pasta, basil from the garden, and good
white wine. I thought it all and made it.
Some days are better than other days.

Some nights I sail in stormy Jonah seas
almost to Crete, and the giant bulls there,
past Cyprus and its goddess and the wake
of the great fish. Mornings I lurch and moan,
finding my land legs, feeling my chest hurt.

The Jews have only borrowed constellations,
live mythlessly beneath a gassy sky.
How do we navigate at night? Perhaps
we don't, we're going nowhere or we've returned.
The broken metaphors of my ship's ribs ache.

I translate poems from Hebrew into English
and make them different. First, I become
the difference, word by word, and hook each line
with artifice. But in the end I know
words don't mean what they say, in any language,

and double misdirections never cancel out.
I've never even scraped my own brain out
and spread it on a page like jam on bread
but that some smeared or tore the paper.
No wonder that my study is a mess.

I have to write about The Scroll of Ruth
because I promised an essay. I shall be wise
and witty, understanding, and very literate.
Readers will understand the Book and I
will pretend, again, to know something I don't.

VI

Poets in Israel regularly pay
thousands of dollars to publish pretty books
no one will ever read, and pay me more
to change them into English. I do myself,
or plan to, and will find a changer to Hebrew,

and shall have neither love nor fame, but I've
a better twiggy nest than the iridescent
sunbird in the garden, and mine has air
conditioning and heating, and fine chairs
stuffed overfull of feathers. They do not shine.

Vision is not enough, I have to see,
too, and hear the children laugh, not just

the still, small voice. My dog barks and snarls
insistent as any angel's whisper and the scent
of shit penetrates as well as incense.

A yellow flowered Datura blooms now, late,
by the rear stone wall. Every part of it
is poisonous. The night odor seduces
the most cautious, chastest passerby. Some
mornings there are bodies, some mornings none.

On Simble, the poetry festivals
last all year beneath the poison trees
and although losers long to nibble leaves,
we've written on each ragged scrap of green
what cannot be digested or erased.

I do not want to go live in my mind, not now
nor in some afterlife. All that I know, I know
from my fat body, toothless, bald, half blind,
and often drunk. Without it soul could only
recombine distortions and mistakes.

VII

Three hours we sat and heard the wisest people —
rabbis, professors, statesmen — all admit
they don't know who they are, in paneled pomp
and glory. They know who Arabs are, who
aren't us, although Israeli. I know who I

am, but I don't understand. My dog has
learned his name, which dogs don't have or men
until we make them singular. Call me a man
and you reduce me, or a Jew, or old.
Naming is killing, murder by distortion.

I shrink or swell, who needs identity?
My cat refuses it, no flower nods
when I say rose. Better to touch than name,
caress than call. And when I say my love
my voice like smoke more hides than shows her there.

God has no name because He can't be killed.
But I am grim. The sky is Mediterranean
blue above the palms, and basil sprouts
next to the crooked walk. My students write
and thrive, and suffer as they must.

My desk's a mess, snuff dust is everywhere
and books I meant to look at weeks ago.
A coffee cup from morning, from last night
a glass that once held whiskey, manuscripts
I have to read and judge pile white as bones.

Darkness seeps in, or maybe light seeps out
late afternoon November, light like thought
uncertain, hard to read by. The time has
number but no name, not twilight or dusk.
There is no sound except attention, hissing.

VIII

Morning is bright, sharp shadows on white stucco
walls, red tiled roofs hot in warm November sun,
late sleep and a hot shower. Later, dinner
with students in Jerusalem, a restaurant
owned by a writer of savage stories.

Simble can't be approached by land or air
because of winds and distances. By sea
the shallow harbor and reefed rocks

require cunning and a master's skill.
The barely purple water coils my feet.

Nobody dies on Simble but I expel
anyone who claims citizenship, or avers
a right to dwell there. Simble is mine
although I understand nothing, or because
this is one of the things I have to know.

I've sometimes lived on Simble since I was
seven, but for years I couldn't find the map,
couldn't explore in love and invitation
the dark stare, the circling encircled arms,
breasts felt relaxed and tightening against me.

I'll rearrange my books, six thousand,
or seven by now, in order of importance.
Now they are subjects, mostly, except where size
imposes. This may take a while, The Bible's easy,
but Shakespeare, Plato, Kant keep lurching

like drunken uncles, babbling all at once
and almost speaking. Poets tumble on the floor,
wrestling and embracing, pages torn,
arrange themselves by color or in shapes
anarchic. The novels are still in boxes.

IX

The craft I sailed away on left behind
a harridan and children and a dog
and many thousand books, and a dry garden
in the desert. I missed some parts for years
and then I didn't, except sometimes near dawn.

Like Job I've more now than before
and like him blink in awe. I think of home,
my parents and a tiny house in Camden,
bad food well burnt, but laughter, love and talk
that mattered. Before the horrid years, the dying.

Father, a cousin, a sister, grandfather,
a son, two friends, in two years. Betrayal
by harridan, time in Beer Sheva, building
a boat and escaping. Map and a bottle
and beautiful friends. Lamb cubes on spits.

Mangos ripen in the back, guavas on the side
of our house. My son writes poetry, my daughter
makes canvas sing. My wife's befriended me
and beautifully mystifies. There's money
to add books, buy booze, and cook for friends.

"Who are you?" ask my peers, and think I'll say
Israeli, Jew, American, right or left.
I am who left Camden, many other
places, sailed from Beer Sheva and arrived
in Simble. I may or may not let you in.

These years before my death my body aches,
what's left of it, and the fuzz of brain
runs crooked. I live here, and I think
that's who I am, who else but Ed Codish,
Yona Mordechai ben Shlomo in Jewish.

X

Nobody dies on Simble, but at the far
west cliffs, where Simble ends, the sea lies dark

and more seductive than unmediated
beauty, naked. My hearing, too, weakens
and the screamed warning fades, is almost gone.

Beyond the edge a boat, gleaming and black
floats lightly on water polished deeply.
The tides and breaking waves are absent here,
the grace of peace apparent in the snarls
of the bears, who gather late, clawing at rocks.

Today I'm at my desk, and my balls itch,
I alternate my lines with a computer game,
push snuff up my nose and wait for dark,
or at least five o'clock and a glass
of whiskey. I'm reading a thriller, brain candy.

The cooking's real enough, I'm good at that,
and gardening and thinking, sometimes.
Simble is only body printed in the brain,
a hymnal so much read the paper crumbles,
yellow and thumb marked, most of the music gone.

The inexactness of the words: no scent
or color on the page has been in the mind,
no finding an idea that matches words
like touch is love, or bite is hunger,
no golden bird, no emperor, no time.

I am a happy man, my wife sits writing
in a room below, my children honor me.
It's time to paint the boat spars blue and set
the shining hull as monument to seas
and streams, crews, and who we really are.

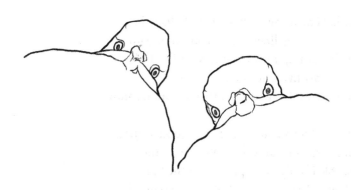

Permissions

"A Juggle of Myrtle Twigs" and "Yetzer Hara"
appeared in *Voices Within the Ark: The Modern Jewish Poets*,
edited by Howard Schwartz and Anthony Rudolf, Avon, New
York, 1980.

Sections of Book i of "Voyage to Gaza" appeared in
The Jerusalem Review, No. 5&6, edited by Gabriel Moked, Tel
Aviv, 2007.

"Emotional Direction" appeared in *Shdemot* 18, edited by
Michael Greenberg, Federation of Kibbutz Movements, Tel Aviv,
1982.

"Lifescape" appeared in *Shdemot* 21-22, edited by Michael
Greenberg, Federation of Kibbutz Movements, Tel Aviv, 1984.

"Aubude" (then entitled "The Poet Approaches Forty")
appeared in *Argo* (Incorporating Delta), Vol. III, No. 1, Argo
Publishing Co., Oxford, 1981.

"Coming Home: Beer Sheva" appeared in *Argo*
(Incorporating Delta), Vol. IV, No. 1, Argo Publishing Co.,
Oxford, 1982.

"Part of an Elegy for Henry Codish" appeared in *Argo*
(Incorporating Delta), Vol. IV, No. 2, Argo Publishing Co.,
Oxford, 1982.

Acknowledgments

What's in my book are dragons, lovers, pigeons,
a landscape scaled to keepsake size, a boat
built of the mind's firm timber seasoned so
it withstood storms and rocky shores and hate
that tried to shipwreck, thwart our voyage ere
it had begun. Now as this odyssey
we've undertaken reaches a port, a haven
safe from heavy seas and hurricanes
Steve Horenstein has taken up the Froglog
and brought it to Yael Shahar to print
with Jacob Yona Horenstein's true drawings
as I and Susann hold the mast and laugh
at all we've weathered, we and dragon friends
and pigeons, phoenixes in a red, green,
and blue flowering garden. My friends
and family gather, the quick and dead
and in these poems I hug flesh and bones
in gratitude that cannot have an end.

About the Poet

ED CODISH WAS born in New York City in 1940 and grew up in the Bronx and Camden, NJ. He studied with Ike Traschen and George Starbuck, receiving his BA from NYU and his MFA from the Writers' Workshop at the University of Iowa. He taught at universities in the US and Israel and at Jewish day schools in Michigan and Massachusetts.

His poems have appeared in numerous Israeli journals and newspapers, including arc, *The Jerusalem Post, Iton 77, Shdemot, Jerusalem Quarterly*, as well as international publications such as *Mosaic* (US), *Whitewater* (US), *Argo* (UK), and *Storie* (Italy). A number of his poems also appeared in the anthology of Jewish verse *Voices Within the Ark*. In addition to his own poetry, he has translated much Hebrew poetry into English.

Ed Codish writes and publishes essays on the religious philosophy of Emmanuel Levinas and other topics, and writes a daily post on current events. He lives in Pardesiya, Israel, with his wife, Susann. Their son, Eitan, is also a published poet. Their daughter, Idit, has published short fiction. A broadsheet poem by Susann hangs over Ed and Susann's bed.

Follow Ed Codish at: www.facebook.com/ed.codish

About the Illustrator

JACOB YONA HORENSTEIN is a Jerusalem artist who creates through painting, illustration, and design. He holds a B.A. in Psychology and Art and is a member of *Hamiffal* (An Artists' Collective). He currently works with a number of companies abroad as an illustrator and designer, with his original designs distributed worldwide. Jacob is also active in producing artistic events and workshops, in addition to teaching drawing classes to students of all ages.

About Kasva Press

"Make its bowls, ladles,
jars and pitchers
with which to offer libations;
make them of pure gold."
(Exodus 25:29)

וְעָשִׂיתָ קְּעָרֹתָיו וְכַפֹּתָיו
וּקְשׂוֹתָיו וּמְנַקִּיֹּתָיו
אֲשֶׁר יֻסַּךְ בָּהֵן
זָהָב טָהוֹר תַּעֲשֶׂה אֹתָם
(שמות פרשת תרומה)

Kasva means "a jar or pitcher". The word appears in the Torah exactly once, where it describes the solid-gold vessels made to hold sacrificial wine and oil in the Tabernacle the Israelites carried with them in their desert wanderings.

We believe that a good book is a vessel for the fluid thoughts of its author — its words, the outpouring of the writer's soul, as precious as the sanctified wine and oil of the Tabernacle.

It is our aim to provide worthy vessels for our authors' creations.